The Beast

The Beast

&

The Pastor

Dag Heward-Mills

Parchment House

Unless otherwise stated, all Scripture quotations are taken from the King James Version of the Bible.

THE BEAUTY, THE BEAST & THE PASTOR

Excerpts from:
John Wesley, Into All the World, by John Telford
(Belfast, Northern Ireland: Ambassador Publications,1999)
Used by permission

First published 2017 by Parchment House
2nd Printing 2018

Find out more about Dag Heward Mills at:

Healing Jesus Campaign
Email: evangelist@daghewardmills.org
Website: www.daghewardmills.org
Facebook: Dag Heward-Mills
Twitter: @EvangelistDag

ISBN : 978-1-68398-193-0

Contents

SECTION 1: WARNINGS

SECTION 2: TYPES OF MARRIAGES

SECTION 3: THE BEASTS OF MARRIAGE

SECTION 4: OVERCOMING IN MINISTRY AND MARRIAGE

Dedication

I dedicate this book to you, my wife Adelaide.
You are my first love and my only love!
If I were to live my life again I would choose you!
When I look around, I cannot find anyone nicer
or better than you!
Thank you for your unique blend of softness and spirituality!
It's been worth living with you!
Thank you for everything!

SECTION 1:

WARNINGS

CHAPTER 1

Warning: Ministry Marriages are Different from Ordinary Marriages

Have ye forgotten the wickedness of your fathers, and the wickedness of the kings of Judah, and THE WICKEDNESS OF THEIR WIVES, and your own wickedness, and THE WICKEDNESS OF YOUR WIVES, which they have committed in the land of Judah, and in the streets of Jerusalem?

Jeremiah 44:9

This book does not apply to you if you are not a pastor.

Do not continue to read this book if you are not a pastor.

If you are not a pastor please stop here!

If you are not a pastor and you continue reading you will criticize things you do not understand.

If you are not a pastor, please get another book on marriage. There are many good books on marriage that will help your life greatly. If you need information on how to get a good book on marriage, please ask at the nearest bookshop.

It is a blessing to have a good marriage and I am aware of many great and good marriages that are marvellous blessings. What are some of the blessings of a great marriage?

1. **A good marriage is a blessing because two are better than one.** There are many scriptures that attest to this fact.

   Two are better than one; because they have a good reward for their labour. For if they fall, the one will lift up his fellow: but woe to him that is alone when he falleth; for he hath not another to help him up.

   Again, if two lie together, then they have heat: but how can one be warm alone? And if one prevail against him, two shall withstand him; and a threefold cord is not quickly broken.

   Ecclesiastes 4:9-12

2. **A good marriage is a blessing because a married couple can do ten times as much as a single person.**

   How should one chase a thousand, and two put ten thousand to flight, except their Rock had sold them, and the Lord had shut them up?

   Deuteronomy 32:30

3. A good marriage is a blessing because a married man has great favour with God.

> Whoso findeth a wife findeth a good thing, and obtaineth favour of the Lord.
>
> Proverbs 18:22

Even though a good marriage is a great blessing, there are many different types of marriages. Not all marriages end up achieving the aim of being a blessing to the couple.

"Counterfeit" marriages only exist because there are real and good marriages.

This book is about certain types of marriages that DO exist. This is a book for pastors and their marriages and NOT for ordinary Christians or non-believers. A large part of this book will not apply to you if you are not a pastor or a pastor's wife.

Many books on marriage make pastors feel that they are married to the wrong person because their marriages are not as nice sounding as the author's.

Then they become shocked when they hear that pastors with such apparently fantastically good marriages are getting divorced.

This is not a book about normal marriages. This book is *not* a balanced two-sided discussion on marital issues. I could indeed write a book about both husbands and wives. I could also write a book about how to have a successful marriage. I could even write a book about how to overcome the various problems that couples face in marriage. However, I am not doing that in this volume. I have chosen to write a book on a topic that is not usually discussed.

This book is about the wickedness of wives. I am writing this book about the wickedness that is submerged beneath the beauty of many wives. If you are looking for a good book on marriage, please find another book, as this is not that book. This book is about the beauty, the beast that is in some pastors' wives and the struggles that pastors have with them. Many pastors marry beauties! But many beauties are also beasts!

I am aware that most people would be afraid to suggest that kind and gentle-looking wives could have any wickedness in them. As I said, I am not intending to have a balanced, two-sided discussion on marriage. If you want a balanced discussion about the good and bad sides of men and the good and bad sides of women, please stop reading now. This is a book about the wickedness of wives, especially the wickedness of some Christian wives and some ministers' wives.

The prophet Jeremiah lamented about the wickedness that wives had committed in Judah and in Jerusalem. These wives were not unbelieving wives but wives that belonged to the house of Israel. The wickedness of the wives that Jeremiah spoke of was the wickedness of idolatry and rebellion against God. The wickedness I am writing about is also about the rebellion of some ministers' wives against God's word.

This, indeed, is a book for ministers and their wives. This is a book that describes some of the experiences that devoted Christians and men of God experience in their marriages. This book is in fact about marital situations that ministers find themselves in, but are unable to talk about.

But and if thou marry, thou hast not sinned; and if a virgin marry, she hath not sinned. Nevertheless SUCH SHALL HAVE TROUBLE in the flesh: but I spare you.

1 Corinthians 7:28

Paul prophesied that those who marry would have trouble in the flesh. Perhaps that is why he did not marry. And by the way, I have not written this book because I do not know any negative things about men. I do! Also, I have not written this book because I want to write negative things about women. I believe so much in the ministry, the anointing, the wisdom and the role of women that I have appointed and promoted many women in ministry. I do not know anyone who has identified and appointed more women as pastors than I have, although I am sure there are others.

As you read on, you may wonder why I do not balance the bad sides of women with the bad sides of men. The reason is simple; that is not the aim of this book! If I were to write about the terrible sins of men in marriage, I would completely miss the message God has given me. If I were to do that, this book would be far bigger than it is and people like you, who do not read much, would not even attempt to read it.

This book is intended to explain some of the mysterious roles women have played in the lives of ministers. We praise our women and are grateful for their role in marriage and ministry. Without the help of women, we would not achieve much in the work of God. I believe that one of the secrets of church growth is to work with women and give them prominence.

Women are praised but little is said about their negative ways, because every one is afraid to look bad or sound as though they have any difficulties in their marriage. But I would not like to keep back anything that may be profitable to you.

... I kept back nothing that was profitable unto you, but have shewed you, and have taught you publicly, and from house to house,

Acts 20:20

The beauty is real but the beast is also real! Little is said about the destructive role of women in ministry. Our Book, the Bible, is not silent on the role of women in the destruction of this world. Through Eve, Adam's life and ministry were destroyed. Through Eve, the whole human race has been sent into darkness and difficulty.

There are many pastors who are in distress, in darkness and in difficulty through their beautiful, well made-up wives.

The reason for this book is to help give the real picture about what some people are experiencing.

Another reason for this book is to help those who are about to choose a "beauty". It is important for them to know that their "beauty" can easily turn into a "beast"! Hopefully, this book will also help all beautiful women not to turn into beasts!

When John Wesley was still single, he fell ill and stayed with a lady who later became his wife. He described how beautiful, how pleasant and how nice she was. Her words were memorable! Her tone was soft! John Wesley was drawn uncontrollably to her comforting love! In his words, Molly, his future wife gave him all the assurances he ever needed. He described her kind of love as intense! He spoke about her "inviolable affection". This English word (inviolable) goes even beyond my ability to interpret. *Eiii!* Inviolable affection! I wish to quote from John Wesley, when he first met his "beauty", his "beloved" Molly (before he married her).

John Wesley said, "I HAD ALL THE ASSURANCES WHICH WORDS COULD GIVE, OF THE MOST INTENSE AND INVIOLABLE AFFECTION."

But one day, after years of marriage he used completely different words to describe her. His beauty had become a beast. One day, his wife was leaving home and embarking on a journey. This is the woman he spoke of having intense inviolable affection for. He said to her as she went out of the door: "I HOPE I NEVER SEE YOUR WICKED FACE AGAIN."

"I hope I never see your wicked face again" was the wish of John Wesley after he had experienced the "beast" in his "beauty". This is a classic example of the pastor who marries a beauty who turns into a beast!

Indeed, this book is also intended to strengthen the arms of those who are deeply embedded in irreversible marriage situations. I hope that this book will help to prevent ministers from divorcing by giving them an understanding of what they are actually experiencing.

I am sure many people will identify things in this book that they can relate with. Use the knowledge, the understanding and the wisdom that you receive from these words to fight the good fight of faith. Marriage is one of the tests we face and we must succeed in it! For some people, marriage is the greatest comfort they will ever have! For some people, marriage is the greatest cross they will ever bear! Some people have excellent marriages. But not all ministers have a good experience or a good story to tell about marriage. Indeed, there are many ministers who would describe their marriage as a battle.

Many great men of God speak about their "excellent marriages" in such a way that intimidates and confuses other Christians and pastors. When other ministers hear their descriptions of their marriages, they shrink away. "Wow," they say to themselves, "I dare not discuss my marriage situation with these blessed ones." (This also happens when pastors attend pastors' conferences and hear fantastic stories about mega churches that have thousands of members.) Most ordinary pastors feel intimidated because they do not have thousands of members attending their churches.

Pastors hear amazing statements from these picture-perfect marriages:

"My wife is the most beautiful woman in the world."

"I owe my life and my ministry to my wife!"

"I don't know where I would be without my wife!"

"There would be no 'me' without 'you'!"

"There is none like you! No one else can touch my heart like you do!"

"I cannot go anywhere without my wife!"

My wife is my greatest assistant, partner and support!"

"I have never quarrelled with my wife before!'

"I tell my wife, 'I love you' ten times every day!"

"I cannot imagine living for even one day without my wife!"

"My wife and I sleep in each other's arms every night!"

"My wife is my closest friend in this world!"

"Whenever I miss my wife, I kiss her picture. But when I see her, I kiss the real thing!"

"My wife is the most beautiful lady in the whole world, my soul mate, my life partner, my friend, my joy, my darling and my heartthrob!"

"If marks were being given for good marriages, I would get 99 per cent!'

Wow! These are wonderful statements! I wish everyone would be able to say all the things above. These are exactly the kinds of marriages we need if we are to succeed in the ministry.

But this is not the experience that all married ministers have! How do I know? I know because I have been in the ministry for many years and I know thousands of pastors. I also know this for a fact because of the rate of divorce amongst pastors. Many ministers have made the statements above, portraying pictures that depict the greatest love of all, only to announce later that they were getting divorced.

For some people, the opposite of all these statements may be more true. There are some pastors who would prefer to say things like:

"My wife is the most beautiful woman in the world, but it is not easy to live with her!'

"I wish I could be delivered from my wife!"

"My wife is the greatest opposer of my life and ministry."

"My wife is the greatest accuser and tormentor of my life!"

"We have not had sex for several months!"

"My wife and I have not been speaking since last month!"

"I don't tell my wife, 'I love you' because I do not want to lie!"

"I can't wait for the day I will be without my wife!"

"My wife and I sleep at opposite ends of the bed every night!"

"I am not close to my wife any more!"

"I do not miss my wife. Whenever I see her picture, I weep for the sorrow in my heart!"

"My marriage is the greatest mistake of my life!"

"If I had a different wife, I would have achieved more in the ministry."

Many of us behave like African herbalists when it comes to marriage. Why do I say so? An African herbalist usually has a single potion that is supposed to cure every ailment you could ever have. This herbalist's potion can cure bad eyesight, piles, toothache, hypertension, diabetes, cancer, rashes, asthma, waist pains, erectile dysfunction, constipation, diarrhoea, general weakness, impotence, etc. You will hear the herbalist advertising his potions and convincing his audience with great zeal. It is only the ignorant who are taken in by claims that one drug can cure all these things. We all know that the same medicine cannot correct your eyesight, your hip pain, your diarrhoea, your skin rashes as well as your high blood pressure and your haemorrhoids.

Yet, when it comes to marriage, most people have one potion that they apply to all marriages. They assume that every marriage is the same and they therefore apply the same measures to every type of marriage. This is a serious mistake because there are different kinds of marriages.

In some cases, you have a very good "devoted husband" who does absolutely everything a husband should do. And sometimes the devoted husband has an equally good wife who does all the things a "devoted" wife could ever do. On the other hand, a devoted husband could have the worst kind of female as his wife. A "devoted" wife could have an evil husband who does not even deserve to have a wife.

Many situations are so varied that they have to be understood on a case-by-case basis. It is wrong to crucify both the good and the bad together on the same day. (Jesus Christ was crucified with thieves and it gave the impression that Jesus Christ was a common thief, simply because He was given the same treatment as a common criminal).

Every marriage gives rise to different experiences. Some people just have to follow the *"Seven steps to a good marriage"* and they will experience great happiness. There are others who can follow *"Seventy steps to a good marriage"*, but will never have happiness.

Indeed, I have met several "unmarriageable" people. They cannot and probably should not marry because they are not suitable for marriage. They simply will never be happy in any marriage situation. Unfortunately, when an "unmarriageable" lady is very beautiful, she is quickly signed in to a marriage and ends up creating an intolerable situation for a pastor. The counselling given to an "unmarriageable" person must be very different from the counselling given to a normal person.

This book is written to give counsel to people who are in certain kinds of marriages. Be careful if you are in one of the good marriage situations because you may be tempted to criticize marriages you do not understand!

Throughout this book I will intentionally not make mention of the personal blessings I have enjoyed in my own marriage. I will also not mention any challenges in my own marriage. Why is that? If I do mention the blessings of my own marriage, you may feel intimidated and think that your marriage is not good. Indeed, if I speak of my own challenges, you may probably not understand them! So just be blessed and receive healing for your life and marriage through the words in these pages.

CHAPTER 2

Warning: The Balance of Power Changes in Ministry Marriages

All things are lawful unto me, but all things are not expedient: all things are lawful for me, BUT I WILL NOT BE BROUGHT UNDER THE POWER OF ANY.

1 Corinthians 6:12

I t is interesting to watch the shifting of the balance of power amongst animals. Watching a herd of elephants and a pride of lions interact will give you a great revelation about how the balance of power can shift from one group to another. In the daytime, the elephants can see clearly and will kill any lion that comes near them. Elephants do not take nonsense from lions during the day.

But as the night falls and darkness descends, the lions can see clearly whilst the elephants cannot. The balance of power now shifts to the lions, which can attack the elephants and actually kill them. Lions have been known to bring down huge elephants in the night when the balance of power has shifted. It is an amazing thing to watch a pride of lions eat a full-grown elephant!

Marriages also experience a shift in the balance of power. There are two ways in which the balance of power can shift.

In a marriage to an unbeliever (*or an "X5" husband – with "A1" being the best*), the balance of power shifts to the man. A non-believing man, or an "X5" husband, is not bound by the Word of God. He is not obedient to the Bible. He will do whatever pleases him. The devoted Christian wife will humbly try to please him to make him change his behaviour. The world is full of stories of husbands who have mistreated their wives. Most laws on divorce favour the woman because women have been mistreated for centuries by unbelieving men.

This book is not about that kind of marriage. This is a book for ministers. If you are not a minister you should not be reading this book because it is not intended for you. Do not criticise what you do not understand. I am also not saying that people in the ministry will have bad marriages. I am saying that the balance of power shifts. The woman has a greater capability to harm the ministry of her husband.

In a marriage to a dedicated pastor and husband (an "A1" husband), the balance of power shifts to the woman. A devoted man of God is bound to obey the Word of God, and so his wife can do almost anything without being divorced. As a result, the balance of power has shifted to the woman, and she can inflict many evils on her "A1" husband. This makes the wife very powerful.

The "A1" pastor has vowed never to divorce or to separate from his wife, no matter what happens! Amazingly, his commitment to marriage gives his wife great power to misbehave. That is the way an employee who can never be sacked behaves. No matter what he does, he will never be dismissed and so he grows in his power and rebellion.

Art thou bound unto a wife? Seek not to be loosed. Art thou loosed from a wife? SEEK NOT A WIFE.

1 Corinthians 7:27

Why would Paul advise a Christian to "seek not a wife"?

Because there are clear dangers involved in giving such power to a woman. Any "A1" man who gets married is giving great power away to his wife. Indeed, it is "A1" devoted men who desperately want to marry. They are usually marrying in an effort to flee fornication and stay morally pure.

Unfortunately, the expectations of devoted "A1" brothers may not be met.

Before marriage, the man of God is powerful and the prospective wife is humble, sweet, gentle, pretty, pleasant and hopeful that she will become the bride of choice.

For the devoted (A1) man of God, when the marriage actually takes place, the balance of power shifts to the woman which is unfortunate. The wife becomes a very powerful force in the minister's life because the balance of power has shifted almost totally into the woman's hand.   She can do almost anything to him and he will be forced to endure it if he does not want to become a divorcee or the husband of two wives.

His wife may not bath, she may not give him food, she may not look nice at home. She may not have sex with him, she may act like a dead body during sex, she may shout at him, she may be rude to him and there will be very little he can do about it! Perhaps, he may give her some persuasive teachings and some counselling. But it is up to her to decide whether she will obey or not. After all, she knows that her "A1" husband will never punish her, never sack her or divorce her!

Why Jesus Did Not Marry

Marriage is a great and risky step for any man of God to take! Marriage by an "A1" pastor is the act of handing over power to a woman who may be far less spiritual than him. That is probably why Jesus did not marry! Marriage by an "A1" pastor is the act of giving power to someone who may not understand your life's mission.

Do you think Jesus would have died on the cross if He had a wife? I do not think so! The wife of Jesus would have opposed the cross. Even Peter opposed the idea of Jesus dying on a cross! If Jesus had married, He would have had quarrels and misunderstandings that would have lowered His anointing.

In spite of these realities, it is not easy for a man of God to remain unmarried. Unfortunately, most unmarried men of God are also suspected of being immoral.

There are many wives who are actually wicked to their devoted (A1) husbands. The wickedness is practiced in secret. It is not easy to see the wickedness of a woman, because it is not the wickedness of committing adultery. It is the wickedness of secret opposition, secret accusations, secret deprivation, secret lovelessness and secret neglect. John Wesley called his wife a wicked woman!

One day, John Wesley said goodbye to his wife Molly. According to his wife, his parting words to her were:

I HOPE I SHALL SEE YOUR WICKED FACE NO MORE.

John Wesley

It is amazing that somebody like John Wesley did not experience the best of marriages. Such an "A1" husband should have had the best of marriages, but that is not the way it was. A devoted (A1) husband will never think of divorce. No matter what he experiences, he will remain in the marriage till the bitter end.

For consider him that endured such CONTRADICTION OF SINNERS against himself, lest ye be wearied and faint in your minds.

Hebrews 12:3

Marriage for an "A1" husband may be the receiving of "contradiction of sinners". When you receive the opposite of what you would expect, you are experiencing the "contradiction of sinners". Jesus also experienced a contradictory response to all His good deeds. He experienced negativity in response to the great love that He showed to mankind. This is why it is said that Jesus received the contradiction of sinners.

CHAPTER 3

Warning: A Warning from the Bible

The thing that hath been, it is that which shall be; and that which is done is that which shall be done: and there is no new thing under the sun. Is there any thing whereof it may be said, see, this is new? It hath been already of old time, which was before us.

Ecclesiastes 1:9-10

Women are *not* often seen as the cause of evil and turmoil in the marriages of ministers. If a woman is openly antagonistic it is easy to identify her as the cause of a marital breakdown. But women, being as beautiful as they are, do not easily give themselves away. Much of the unsuspecting public sympathize with beautiful and harmless-looking wives.

Adultery by a man is hardly ever connected to his wife's poor sexual performances or her bad attitude at home. However, this may be the real cause of the adulterous affair.

Senior pastors do not often r*ebuke, correct, oppose and restrict* wives who cause marital problems. Badly behaved wives must be rebuked, corrected, opposed and restricted. The failure to openly rebuke, openly correct and openly restrict women who destroy men of God in their marriages, leads to the strengthening of these women.

> And Memucan answered before the king and the princes, Vashti THE QUEEN HATH NOT DONE WRONG TO THE KING ONLY, BUT ALSO TO ALL THE PRINCES, AND TO ALL THE PEOPLE that are in all the provinces of the king Ahasuerus. For this deed of the queen shall come abroad unto all women, so that they shall despise their husbands in their eyes, when it shall be reported, The king Ahasuerus commanded Vashti the queen to be brought in before him, but she came not. Likewise shall the ladies of Persia and Media say this day unto all the king's princes, which have heard of the deed of the queen. Thus shall THERE ARISE TOO MUCH CONTEMPT AND WRATH.
>
> If it please the king, let there go a royal commandment from him, and let it be written among the laws of the Persians and the Medes, that it be not altered, That Vashti come no more before king Ahasuerus; and let the king give her royal estate unto another that is better than she. And when the king's decree which he shall make shall be

published throughout all his empire, (for it is great,) ALL THE WIVES SHALL GIVE TO THEIR HUSBANDS HONOUR, BOTH TO GREAT AND SMALL.

Esther 1:16-20

Memucan was concerned about allowing Vashti's wrong behaviour to go unnoticed and uncorrected. Today, the misbehaviour of many wives goes uncorrected. People are afraid to say negative things about the "First Lady of the church". Because of this, "much contempt and wrath" has risen up in the body of Christ.

Instead of being rebuked for doing evil, these women are even further glorified and are magnified before the public. The deceptive glorification of bad wives only serves to strengthen the works of darkness that hinders the ministry. Husbands are simply encouraged to love their wives as they are. No one is bold enough to say anything other than "Husbands love your wives." Many women are therefore not corrected and neither are they led into the paths of righteousness.

In some places, Fathers' Day is used to rebuke irresponsible fathers and call them to order whilst Mothers' Day is used to celebrate mothers and praise them for their good works. Unfortunately, there is an assumption that the man must be a wrong doer in every marriage. In this chapter, I want you to look into the Bible and see what the Word of God can tell us about this. Have wives played an evil role when left unchecked? Here is a warning from history and a warning from the Bible!

1. **A warning from Adam:**

    Adam had the greatest authority and was entrusted with the responsibility of naming all the animals in this world. His whole ministry and relationship with God was destroyed when he yielded to pressure coming from his wife. Most of the curses in this world therefore came through a man yielding to pressure from a wife. Indeed, Eve was not in charge of this world; but she was the influence behind the man who was in charge. She pushed him, she manipulated him and she pressured him to go against the God who had made man the supreme ruler of the earth.

And unto Adam he said, Because thou hast hearkened unto THE VOICE OF THY WIFE, and hast eaten of the tree, of which I commanded thee, saying, Thou shalt not eat of it: cursed is the ground for thy sake; in sorrow shalt thou eat of it all the days of thy life.

Genesis 3:17

I once watched a documentary on a sixteen-year-old girl who influenced her twenty-one year old boyfriend to murder her father and her mother. Her mother was murdered in the morning and her father was murdered in cold blood in the afternoon. During her trial she claimed innocence and pointed out that her boyfriend had committed the murders. In the end, her boyfriend was given a twenty-year sentence and she was given a sentence of forty years. She was interviewed later and in the interview, lamented that things had gone wrong and that blame had been unduly put on her.

She made a remarkable statement that I think all husbands should take note of. *She said her boyfriend should have known better than to have listened to her!* She agreed that she pressurized her boyfriend to kill her parents so that they could be together, but insisted that *he should have known better than to listen to her and murder her parents.*

If Adam had known better than to listen to Eve, perhaps we would all not be in the mess we are in today!

If you are a man of God in a place of authority, you must be very careful of the influence your wife has on you. Your allegiance is to God! You must obey Him and not your wife. It is a tragic leadership mistake to obey your wife rather than the One who called you!

2. A warning from Abraham:

And Sarai said unto Abram, Behold now, the Lord hath restrained me from bearing: I PRAY THEE, GO IN UNTO MY MAID; it may be that I may obtain children by her. And Abram hearkened to the voice of Sarai.

Genesis 16:2

Abraham was entrusted with the mission of producing Isaac. Under pressure from his wife, he had a child with Hagar and produced Ishmael. Abraham had the affair with Hagar because of a domestic discussion or argument he had with Sarai.

Similarly today, many ministers have affairs with other women because of what happens in their homes. One conversation in Abraham's home resulted in all the difficulties and problems we have today in the Middle East. If Abraham had known better than to listen to Sarah, perhaps we would not have many of the world crises that we have today.

3. A warning from Job:

But he said unto her, THOU SPEAKEST AS ONE OF THE FOOLISH WOMEN speaketh. What? Shall we receive good at the hand of God, and shall we not receive evil? In all this did not Job sin with his lips.

Job 2:10

On the other hand, Job knew better than to listen to his wife and rebuked her strongly when she suggested that he should forsake his God.

Job was a man who feared God. He was a man of patience, a man of wisdom and a man who was proved right in the end. In his great wisdom and patience, he rebuked his wife with a famous rebuke that is recorded for all to see.

Unlike Adam and Abraham, Job called his wife a foolish woman!

Can you imagine how different the world would have been if Adam had called Eve a foolish woman and refused to obey her?

Can you imagine how different the world would have been if Abraham had called Sarah a foolish woman and refused to obey her?

Can you imagine how different your ministry would be if you would only call your wife a foolish woman and refuse to obey her influence when she is being a foolish woman?

Job refused to be influenced, coerced and pressurized into the wrong direction. He was a good moral husband and claimed that he had never looked at another woman lustfully. Listen to what he said: *"I made a covenant with mine eyes; why then should I think upon a maid?" (Job 31:1).* Imagine that! He was deeply committed to his marriage. Yet, he stood firmly and resisted his wife when she behaved foolishly. He gave her a strong rebuke, calling her foolish, which is what she was!

From today do not be afraid of rebuking your wife when you have to. Don't be afraid of rebuking somebody else's wife when she is being foolish. Don't be a man pleaser. The marriage of a minister is different from that of an ordinary Christian. You are a man of authority, so obey the Lord and not your wife. Don't take any notice of those who claim they have these picture-perfect marriages.

Some people love to give a good show of unreal things. It is called "PDA" (Public Display of Affection). Talk to many ministers and ask them to speak honestly about their marriages. You will discover that many people around you have had the experiences of Job, Abraham and Adam.

4. A warning from Jesus:

For there are some eunuchs, which were so born from their mother's womb: and there are some eunuchs, which were made eunuchs of men: and there be eunuchs, which have made themselves eunuchs for the kingdom of heaven's sake. He that is able to receive it, let him receive it.

Matthew 19:12

The fact that Jesus did not marry, should be the greatest warning of all time. If marriage was the perfect will of God, Jesus would have married and demonstrated to us why and how it should be done. We would have learnt from Jesus' example of a perfect marriage. But Jesus did not marry. Why not? Jesus stayed unmarried because of His mission.

If Jesus had married, His wife would have resisted His going to the cross just as Peter did. His wife would have said, "Think about us. What will happen to us? What will happen to Your son?" Perhaps, Jesus would have been influenced to travel out to India to finish His ministry there. Every married person is somehow influenced by their marriage. The women in Jesus' life simply ministered to Him but He did not marry them. He knew better than to come under the influence of a woman. Jesus was the second Adam, the wiser Adam!

5.   A warning from Paul:

But by the grace of God I am what I am: and his grace which was bestowed upon me was not in vain; but I laboured more abundantly than they all: yet not I, but the grace of God which was with me.

1 Corinthians 15:10

You will notice that Apostle Paul bore more fruit than all the other apostles. He worked harder and reached further than any of the others. Perhaps, it is because he did not get married that he was able to bear so much fruit. Today, we quote from Apostle Paul's writings far more than any of the other disciples who had actually walked with Jesus.

The apostle Paul confirmed that it would be better not to marry for the sake of ministry. Paul wished that all of us would be able to stay unmarried and minister the word of God. Unfortunately, that would be too difficult for most of us ordinary humans. Mercy!

For I would that all men were even as I myself. But every man hath his proper gift of God, one after this manner, and another after that.

1 Corinthians 7:7

But and if thou marry, thou hast not sinned; and if a virgin marry, she hath not sinned. Nevertheless SUCH SHALL HAVE TROUBLE IN THE FLESH: but I spare you.

1 Corinthians 7:28

Apostle Paul warned that all those who married would have trouble. What kind of trouble? One basketful of troubles belongs to all those who venture into marriage. Don't believe those who give you a rosy picture of everything. There is nothing rosy in this world of futility!

Paul advocated that women have a covering to protect them from evil spirits. There are spirits without bodies seeking to enter and influence women. Without a covering, our women are exposed to these evil spirits.

For this cause ought the woman to have power on her head because of the angels.

1 Corinthians 11:10

Many women who are elevated to positions of high spiritual authority and do not have a covering, are exposed to a terrible influence of evil spirits.

There were giants in the earth in those days; and also after that, when THE SONS OF GOD CAME IN UNTO THE DAUGHTERS OF MEN, and they bare children to them, the same became mighty men which were of old, men of renown.

Genesis 6:4

According to this scripture, the spirits had intercourse with the daughters of men and gave birth to monsters. This is what happens when there is an unholy and illegitimate interaction between evil spirits and women. It is to protect women from contact with these evil influences that they need a covering.

When a man is married to a woman and she disrespects him, she moves out of his covering. She elevates herself when she challenges him. She elevates herself when she opposes him. She elevates herself when she fights him. She moves out of her covering when she stands toe to toe with him as an equal. Because of this equalization in marriage, many husbands provide no covering for their wives.

Equalization is the act of rising to the level of your cover, effectively removing yourself from the canopy that should have been over you.

Sometimes, ministers' wives who preach and teach become difficult to control because they are elevated above the covering over them. You would have thought that when women study the Word of God it would make them better wives and better helpers of the man of God. Not so! The statistics we have reveal the opposite.

Which of these Two Wives Do You Prefer?

I once spoke to a pastor who had had the privilege of marrying two different women at two different times of his life. I asked him which of the two ladies he preferred.

Without any hesitation he said, "I prefer the marriage to the lady who was _not_ preaching, holding conferences or writing books. When I was married to the one who was not a preacher, we had a normal life and she was pleasant to live with. I had no one challenging my authority from day to day."

He continued, "My wife who was a preacher was deceptive; challenging, accusing, fighting and opposing me continually. She launched her own books and continually challenged my authority and leadership."

Yes, it is a great thing for women to preach. But there are great dangers for the women who preach. They often "grow out" of the canopy and covering and become exposed to evil spirits.

When the evil spirits interact with them, they turn into monsters and become even more cantankerous.

For this cause ought the woman to have power on her head because of the angels.

1 Corinthians 11:10

CHAPTER 4

Warning: A Warning from History

Look unto Abraham your father, and unto Sarah that bare you: for I CALLED HIM ALONE, and blessed him, and increased him.

Isaiah 51:2

The call of God is a lonely call. It is lonely because you are called alone. All through the Bible, you will not find God calling *groups* of people. You do not even find God calling *couples* to work for Him.

None of the patriarchs whom God used had one wife. God did not use any of them as specially anointed couples in the Bible. Abraham, Isaac, Jacob, David, Solomon and Saul all had a number of wives and different groups of children. It appears that one woman was not able to cater for the needs of these men.

The call of Moses, the call of Samuel, the call of David, the call of Solomon, Abraham and Isaac, were all individual events. No one was called as a married couple.

On the other hand, we as Christians present couples as though they were called together by God. It is as though they were raised up and anointed together from the womb to serve God as a team.

We also present committees and councils to God for His blessing. But God never called a committee or a council! God never called a couple! When couples have worked together nicely, each of them had an individual call. Committees and councils are set up because human beings do not trust each other enough to give a lot of power to any one person.

Why is all this important? It is important because many people do not realise that God is working with *a man* that He has chosen. Whether you join to help the man or not does not really matter. It is the person whom God has called that really matters. With or without an associate, a wife, a friend, a helper or a co-minister, the call of God will go on. Once God has purposed a thing, nothing can disannul it.

This is the purpose that is purposed upon the whole earth: and this is the hand that is stretched out upon all the nations.

For the Lord of hosts hath purposed, and WHO SHALL DISANNUL IT? and his hand is stretched out, and who shall turn it back?

Isaiah 14:26-27

A Warning from an Evangelist

According to one evangelist, there was a man who was assisting him by praying for the sick during his crusades. The evangelist would preach and this man would pray for the sick. One day, this man decided to leave the team. This was a big blow to the evangelist, who would now have to learn how to pray for the sick himself. Apparently, when this man was leaving, he told someone, "The evangelist is finished!" Perhaps he thought that his departure would deal the deathblow to the evangelist's ministry.

I want you to remember the Scripture in Isaiah 51 about Abraham; *"I called him alone."* God does not call groups! God did not call an evangelistic team. God called the evangelist! After this man left the ministry, the evangelist's ministry flourished and became a worldwide ministry.

A Warning from a Healer

I know another great healer whose wife left him unceremoniously. He woke up one morning and found a message that she was leaving him. In one of their heated arguments, she said to him, "I will finish you. I will destroy you." She really thought that her departure would be the end of this healer's ministry. To her surprise, the healer's ministry continued successfully after her departure.

A Warning from a Great Pastor

I know another great pastor who had a huge church and a thriving international ministry. He had great conflicts with his wife. At a point, divorce became inevitable. Her husband described to me how he begged her not to leave him. She also said to him, "I will finish you!"

She was so convinced that her departure would finish off the great pastor's ministry that she asked to be paid her divorce settlement before the announcement of their divorce was made public. She felt that the announcement would cause the ministry to crash and there would be no money to settle her. However, after she was paid and the divorce announced, this great pastor continued to flourish and his ministry became even bigger. This rebellious wife was unable to "finish off" her husband's ministry.

A Warning from the Two Goliaths

I remember another pastor who had two mighty assistants nicknamed "the two Goliaths." These two Goliaths and their senior pastor seemed to be a mighty spiritual triad whom God was using in their nation. Unfortunately after many years, cracks began to appear in the triad and there was a great strife that caused them to split up and go their separate ways.

As the years went by, the two Goliaths fizzled out into nothingness. However the original pastor, who was the leader, went forward and became very great. The two Goliaths mistakenly thought they could destroy their leader's ministry.

Remember the prophecy of Isaiah! *"I called you alone."* God does not call people in groups of three, groups of five, groups of seven or groups of nine. He calls people alone! Your presence or absence from someone who is called, does not change what God will do. It is a great deception to think that someone's ministry depends on your presence or absence.

I have a whole lot of people around me in the ministry. Some of them do what I say and some do not. Some obey me and some do not. But God called me alone. Their presence, their obedience or their absence, will not change anything.

A Warning from William Carey

William Carey, known as the father of modern missions, was a missionary to India. He is the person who inspired the worldwide church to begin sending missionaries to the ends of the world. He translated the Bible into Bengali and twenty-nine other languages, printed the Bibles and supplied them to hundreds of thousands of Asians.

He was married to three different women during his ministry in India. His first wife was called Dolly. She was six years older than him and uneducated. William Carey married her whilst he was a teenager and a new Christian. Dolly knew very little of the Lord herself.

His first marriage to Dolly was very difficult because he was married to an unwilling, rebellious, accusative and mentally unstable woman. She was very difficult to be with on the mission field. Initially, she did not even want to go along with her husband to the mission field, nor allow their children to accompany their father. She only went along after much pleading. Their marriage was also further affected by her bouts of depression and later, mental illness, following the loss of three of their children to disease.

In her mentally unstable state, she would accuse her husband of having affairs with women, including their closest friends and the mission's servants. After twelve years of suffering from delusional paranoia, Dolly died. They were married for twenty-six years.

Six months after she died, William Carey married Charlotte, a Danish countess who lived next door to the mission. They were both forty-six years old. She was a petite, well-educated woman, fluent in seven languages and a supporter of the missionary work. In her teen years she had been severely burned in a fire that had injured her legs.

Though she had to spend much of her day resting, she was an enormous encouragement to her husband. She helped him with his challenging translation work and their growing ministry. Their thirteen years of marriage were happy ones. William Carey was happiest with this second wife; and when he was dying, he requested to be buried by his second wife who had made him the happiest. He clearly did not want to lie by his first wife, even as a dead body.

William Carey married Grace, his third wife, after a period of mourning. She was a forty-five year old widow who loved the Lord and served faithfully beside Carey in the ministry. Grace lovingly cared for Carey during their eleven years together.

As you can see the presence or absence of any of these women did not in any way prevent William Carey from fulfilling his calling. He was not called as part of a group. He was called alone!

In fact, his first wife did not even want to go on the mission with him. Each woman that was attached to him was privileged to be part of the great mission that was accomplished. But it was he, William Carey, who was called and set apart for modern missions. God called William Carey alone.

A Warning from Adoniram Judson

Adoniram Judson was a great missionary to Burma. He had a great burden to go to Burma and labour for the people of Burma (present day Myanmar). He became "the father of American missions", being the first American citizen to become a foreign missionary. Judson's vision was to translate the Bible directly from the Hebrew and Greek into the Burmese language. He worked on the translation for twenty-eight years, and with such precision that his translation is still used in Myanmar today. He was also married three times and had three wonderful women at his side for three different seasons of his life.

In his years in Burma, Adoniram Judson saw thousands of lives transformed in Christ. He also faced years of persecution, imprisonment and family tragedy.

Adoniram's first wife was Ann. She felt willing to spend her days in heathen lands with her husband and give up all her comforts to go where God saw fit to send her. They first went to India, but Adoniram was set on going to Burma.

They arrived in Burma to find a country with Buddhism as the only allowed religion. Adoniram worked for hours each day to become an expert in the language. Ann, on the other hand, exercised her gift of hospitality in Burma and through that became more fluent in understanding and speaking the Burmese of the common citizen.

Six years after arriving in Rangoon, Judson conducted his first public Christian service. Following a threat of war between Britain and the Burmese emperor, Adoniram was thrown into prison for seventeen months. Prisoners were not given food and many starved to death. A prisoner could only get food from friends who visited and prisoners underwent special torture sessions in the prison. Ann went to see every important person she could to help secure the release of Adoniram.

After his release from prison, Ann became sick. Whilst Adoniram was away in another city doing some important translation work, Ann collapsed and died. Not too long after he got back home, their little daughter also died after a bout of dysentery.

Adoniram continued his work of translating the Burmese Bible and in 1834, at the age of forty-six, he finished translating the whole Bible. This was twenty-one years after he and Ann had arrived in Burma as missionaries.

Eight years after Ann died, it was time for Adoniram to get his second wife. Adoniram married Sarah who was a young widow of another missionary and had continued in the field after her husband died. Adoniram and Sarah began a vibrant ministry life together.

Sarah suffered from dysentery and the doctors insisted that the only way to recover was a sea voyage to America; away from the terrible heat and the parasites in the tropics. Sarah died during the journey and was buried on the island of St Helena.

It was time for the third wife. Whilst looking for a biographer to write Sarah's life story, Adoniram was introduced to Emily who had a great deal of writing talent. She was twenty-seven years old, half Adoniram's age and had harboured a desire to become a foreign missionary. Adoniram proposed marriage to Emily within a month and they were married the following June.

They went back to Burma and Adoniram worked to complete a Burmese-English dictionary for new missionaries entering Burma. There were, by this time, thirty-six thriving Baptist churches.

Adoniram later caught a severe cold accompanied by a high fever. Dysentery followed and Adoniram had to spend most of his time in bed. As he grew worse, doctors recommended another sea voyage. Emily booked him on a French ship, which was sailing to the Isle of France. She could not go with him because she was advanced in her second pregnancy. Before setting sail he confided in his wife that, "I am not tired of my work. Neither am I tired of this world. Yet when Christ calls me home, I shall go with the gladness of a boy bounding away from his school. Death will never take me by surprise; I feel so strong in Christ!"

Adoniram died during the journey and was buried at sea, three weeks before Emily delivered their child. It took three months for her to receive word of Adoniram's passing. Four years later, she also passed away.

The presence or absence of each of these three wives did not in any way destroy Adoniram Judson's mission to Burma. As you can see, Adoniram Judson was not called with any particular woman.

He was called alone and three women were privileged to be attached to him for three different seasons of his life! Always remember the prophecy of Isaiah.

A warning from John Wesley

After the early church movement, one of the greatest ever movements to rise was Methodism, founded by John Wesley. John Wesley struggled with his violent, fighting, challenging and accusing wife from the day he entered into marriage with her.

Because she was loud and open about her confrontation and unhappiness with John Wesley, the story of his marriage is known by many. All the titanic struggles of John Wesley's life and ministry had to do with his dreadful marriage. Perhaps John Wesley would have achieved much more for the Lord if he had not been married to this difficult woman.

A warning from marriages all around

History shows that many pastors have had serious marital problems. We know about these problems when the final announcement comes that they are to be divorced.

When the final announcement comes, we find out that they have been living with intractable problems for many years. Some of the divorcing pastors have been at the brink of divorce many times but managed to swing back just in time.

Often, no one is aware of what is going on, because they constantly present the picture of a blissful marriage. They often leave ordinary Christians wishing that their marriages were as good as the man of God's seemingly perfect marriage.

Thank God for blissful marriages. There are indeed many pastors who have blissful marriages. But do not be deceived that all is rosy. Today, when people encounter a few challenges, they think of divorce. Apostle Paul did not present a rosy or easy picture of marriage. He said, "But and if thou marry, thou hast not sinned; and if a virgin marry, she hath not sinned. *Nevertheless such shall have trouble* in the flesh: but I spare you" (1 Corinthians 7:28).

I recently heard the testimony of a daughter of a very, very great man of God. I shall not mention his name here, but you know of him very well. This daughter was experiencing great difficulties in her marriage.

She told her husband, "My parents never had such problems. There is something terribly wrong with our marriage."

As her marital problems multiplied, she went to her parents and confided in them. For the first time, her parents revealed that they had had the same marital problems that she was having.

They told her, "We never argued in front of you children. We never let you know when we were having challenges."

The daughter was amazed. "But we never saw any kind of problem in your marriage." But her parents insisted, "We had all those problems. You just didn't know because we did not want you to know."

People have problems that they are not sharing. Do not curse yourself because you do not have a perfect situation. Just assume that things are hidden from you. Your marriage is probably better than that of others.

Conclusion

The fact that you are married to someone does not mean God called you with the person. My wife was not with me when God called me. God called me when I was an unmarried student. I was called to the ministry and started working for the Lord long before I got married. I founded my church before I got married. It is possible that I was even called before I was born.

Before I formed thee in the belly I knew thee; and before thou camest forth out of the womb I sanctified thee, and I ordained thee a prophet unto the nations.

Jeremiah 1:5

Getting married did not change my calling into a "joint calling". The nice family picture that perfect couples present, gives the impression that they have a joint call. This is a delusion that only comes along with many great dangers.

It deceives the assistants, the wives and associates that they are more important than they actually are. It causes them to challenge the one who is called. It feeds a deception that they can destroy or finish off the man of God.

Most rebellious top associates and wives launch out based on this delusion. If you understand the message of this chapter, you will never think you can destroy someone whom God has called. Your presence or your absence cannot change God's plan.

CHAPTER 5

Warning: Terror Warnings from Solomon

Her house is the way to hell, going down to the chambers of death.

Proverbs 7:27

S olomon had many warnings about relating to women. Solomon should know a thing or two, having had relations with a thousand women. He used several terrifying descriptions of wrong relationships with women. It is important to take these terrifying warnings from Solomon seriously.

Perhaps, it is the possibility of entering into such terrifying relationships that prevented our Lord Jesus from ever getting married. Apostle Paul, the most fruitful of the apostles, also never attempted to get married. It is interesting that Apostle Paul bore more fruit than all the other married apostles.

Let us now go through the descriptions of a marriage that Solomon warned us about.

The descriptions from Solomon reveal the terrifying realities of being married to the wrong woman.

Solomon taught that marriage to an unknown person is very dangerous. *Marriage to a stranger releases the terrifying experiences of the unknown.* Not knowing whom you are marrying may be the door to a life of hell for you.

> Say unto wisdom, Thou art my sister; and call understanding thy kinswoman: That they may keep thee from THE STRANGE WOMAN from the STRANGER which flattereth with her words.
>
> Proverbs 7:4-5

1. Solomon declared: Marriage to a stranger can lead to being married to a person who is subtle of heart. You never know what she is really thinking and what her real mind is about anything.

> And, behold, there met him a woman with the attire of an harlot, and SUBTIL OF HEART.
>
> Proverbs 7:10

2. Solomon declared: Marriage to a strange woman can lead to having a loud and unyielding woman at your side. She will never agree to anything. She will never say yes, she

will never say no, she will never agree, she will never bend, she will never bow, she will never do what you want her to do.

She is loud and stubborn; her feet abide not in her house:

Proverbs 7:11

3. Solomon declared: Marriage to a stranger can lead to having someone who does not like to stay at home. You will not have all the things you thought you would receive in your home because you did not marry a homely person.

Now is she WITHOUT, now IN THE STREETS, and lieth in wait at every corner.

Proverbs 7:12

4. Solomon declared: Marriage to a stranger can lead to being married to someone who is impudent. She will be arrogant, she will be rude and pushy.

So she caught him, and kissed him, and with an IMPUDENT FACE said unto him,

Proverbs 7:13

5. Marriage to a stranger will give the terrifying experiences of being in a slaughterhouse. You will be slaughtered like an ox! Your life will be destroyed because of your marriage. I am sure you never imagined being slaughtered through marriage.

He goeth after her straightway, AS AN OX GOETH TO THE SLAUGHTER, or as a fool to the correction of the stocks;

Proverbs 7:22

6. Marriage to a stranger sets you up for the chilling experiences of getting married into a life of correction. You will never be allowed to play, relax or be happy. Your home will be the home of a strict headmistress with a cane.

You will never be yourself. You will never unwind! You will never relax!

He goeth after her straightway, as an ox goeth to the slaughter, or as a fool TO THE CORRECTION of the stocks;

Proverbs 7:22

7. Marriage to a stranger brings you close to a woman who has destroyed many men. She has had relationships with many men. Men have been wounded by falling prey to her charms and falling into her arms. Many strong men have been slain by her. You married a slayer of men and you are the next candidate to be slain.

For she hath cast down many wounded: yea, MANY STRONG MEN HAVE BEEN SLAIN BY HER.

Proverbs 7:26

8. Marriage to a strange woman is the terrifying experience of going to hell. As soon as you sign the marriage register, you enter the lift and descend 97 floors into the belly of the earth. There, you will burn, fry, bake, sizzle and be grilled by your wife until death do you part.

Her house is the way to HELL, going down to the chambers of death.

Proverbs 7:27

Should you be surprised when people jump out of hell? If you see a man taking a lift and coming from ninety-seven floors below, where the fires are raging, would you ask, "O man of God why are you coming out of hell fire? Why do you not stay there for fifteen more years?"

If a marriage can be compared to hell, should you be surprised that people would want to jump out of such a marriage? Should you be surprised if people actually jump out of these marriages? Dear friend, not every one can stay in hell. There are many men of God who will be able to submit themselves

40

to the experience of hell-marriages for the rest of their lives. But others will simply take the lift and come all the way out from the 97th floor in the belly of the earth. They need some fresh air and they need to escape.

If you do not accept these Scriptures, you will not understand why some people get divorced. The Word of God is true and marriages and relationships that are like hell do exist.

Marriage to a stranger takes you directly into the horrors of a chamber of death. Death is a terrible experience. It is the saddest experience human beings encounter during their stay on earth.

To say that your relationship with a woman is the same as going into the chambers of death is the most terrifying warning I have ever heard of! Do you want to live your life in a mortuary, in a coffin or by the dead? I don't think so!

These warnings from Solomon must be taken seriously. There are people who are experiencing the "chambers of death marriage", just as Solomon described. Watch out! Beware of the woman you know little about! Beware of the strange woman! Beware of the stranger!

CHAPTER 6

Warning: Women Can Be Used As Weapons

And the Lord God said unto the woman, What is this that thou hast done? And the woman said, The serpent beguiled me, and I did eat.

Genesis 3:13

Women have done great things for God and the Lord will use them even more in the future. The Holy Spirit has been poured out on both the sons and the daughters. This notwithstanding, the Bible gives us a long list of women who have been used as weapons of destruction.

The subject of this chapter is to understand how women have been used as weapons to destroy God's work. It is important for a minister of the gospel to recognize that women are likely to be used as weapons to destroy his life and ministry. *Women who can destroy you range from strange women whom you hardly know to women whom you know very well, such as your wife!*

Let me share with you several examples from the Bible. Below is a list of ways in which women have been used to afflict great men.

1. THE DESTRUCTION OF ADAM: A woman brought down the very first man. A wife, the only woman in the world, was used as a bridge to gain access to the only man in the world. By causing her to fall, satan gained access to Adam. Adam tried to help his wife but landed in the same difficulty as she did. Eve was used as a bridge. Satan gained access to Adam, the head of the created world through his wife Eve. Satan destroyed man by using his wife.

    And when the woman saw that the tree was good for food, and that it was pleasant to the eyes, and a tree to be desired to make one wise, she took of the fruit thereof, and did eat, and gave also unto her husband with her; and he did eat.

    Genesis 3:6

2. THE DESTRUCTION OF JOSEPH: Through a woman, one of the heroes in the Bible was given a prison sentence. A lying woman was used to damage Joseph's life. Through Potiphar's wife, Joseph went to prison and spent a long time in captivity.

And it came to pass, when his master heard the words of his wife, which she spake unto him, saying, After this manner did thy servant to me; that his wrath was kindled.

And Joseph's master took him, and put him into the prison, a place where the king's prisoners were bound: and he was there in the prison.

Genesis 39:19-20

3. THE DESTRUCTION OF KING DAVID: There was a snare for the man after God's heart and that snare was a woman. A bride, was used as a weapon against king David. The plan was to use David's love for Michal to gain access to him.

    And Saul said, I will give him her, THAT SHE MAY BE A SNARE TO HIM, AND that the hand of the Philistines may be against him. Wherefore Saul said to David, Thou shalt this day be my son in law in the one of the twain.

    1 Samuel 18:21

4. THE DESTRUCTION OF SAMSON: The captivity and death of God's strongest man was accomplished by a woman. A girlfriend was used as a weapon in the life and ministry of Samson. Delilah was used as a weapon to gain access to Samson, the leader of the Israelite nation. Through Delilah, Samson was destroyed, blinded and silenced.

    And it came to pass afterward, that he loved a woman in the valley of Sorek, whose name was Delilah. And the lords of the Philistines came up unto her, and said unto her, ENTICE HIM, and see wherein his great strength lieth, and by what means we may prevail against him, THAT WE MAY BIND HIM to afflict him: and we will give thee every one of us eleven hundred pieces of silver. And Delilah said to Samson, Tell me, I pray thee, wherein thy great strength lieth, and wherewith thou mightest be bound to afflict thee.

    Judges 16:4-6

44

5. THE DESTRUCTION OF SOLOMON BY WOMEN: The destruction of the wisest man on earth was achieved only by women. Wives and concubines were used as weapons in the life of Solomon. The subtle influence of Solomon's wives was the power that neutralized the great wisdom of Solomon. All the wisdom that God gave to Solomon was destroyed by these wives.

But king Solomon loved many strange women, together with the daughter of Pharaoh, women of the Moabites, Ammonites, Edomites, Zidonians, and Hittites;

Of the nations concerning which the LORD said unto the children of Israel, Ye shall not go in to them, neither shall they come in unto you: for surely they will turn away your heart after their gods: Solomon clave unto these in love.

And he had seven hundred wives, princesses, and three hundred concubines: and his wives turned away his heart.

For it came to pass, when Solomon was old, that his wives turned away his heart after other gods: and his heart was not perfect with the LORD his God, as was the heart of David his father.

1 Kings 11:1-4

6. THE DESTRUCTION OF STRONG MEN BY WOMEN: The slaying of strong men is blamed on the strange woman. Strange and unknown women are described as hunters in the book of Proverbs. These hunters are to destroy a man and turn him into a piece of bread. Under the influence of the strange woman, a great man is turned into an ox in the slaughter house. The wounded and the strong are destroyed by strange women.

For she hath cast down many wounded: yea, many strong men have been slain by her. Her house is the way to hell, going down to the chambers of death.

Proverbs 7:26-27

7. THE DESTRUCTION OF ARMIES BY WOMEN: Entire armies have been corrupted by women. Daughters were used as weapons in the wars described by the prophet Daniel. They were sent as weapons to neutralise and to fight the enemy. Many people do not go to war because of their love for women. Mark Anthony who fought to be the leader of Rome was mocked because of his love for Cleopatra.

He shall also set his face to enter with the strength of his whole kingdom, and upright ones with him; thus shall he do: and HE SHALL GIVE HIM THE DAUGHTER OF WOMEN, CORRUPTING HER: but she shall not stand on his side, neither be for him.

Daniel 11:17

8. THE DESTRUCTION OF PROPHETS BY WOMEN: A fornicating woman is described as having destroyed the ministries of many prophets and saints. In her was found the blood of many prophets. She has destroyed many men of God.

Rejoice over her, thou heaven, and ye holy apostles and prophets; for God hath avenged you on her.
And IN HER WAS FOUND THE BLOOD OF PROPHETS, and of saints, and of all that were slain upon the earth.

Revelation 18:20, 24

9. THE DESTRUCTION OF THE REDEEMED BY WOMEN: The defilement of the redeemed is by women. Women are used to defile the saints. The presence and effect of these women, somehow, defiled the church.

These are they, which were not DEFILED WITH WOMEN; for they are virgins. These are they which follow the Lamb whithersoever he goeth. These were redeemed from among men, being the firstfruits unto God and to the Lamb.

Revelation 14:4

10. THE DESTRUCTION OF KINGS BY WOMEN: Women have destroyed many kings. Amazingly many wrong decisions taken by authority figures are influenced by women.

Give not thy strength unto women, nor thy ways to that which DESTROYETH KINGS.

Proverbs 31:3

11. THE DESTRUCTION OF MEN OF GOD BY WOMEN: According to the Bible, there is trouble waiting for those who get married. Marriage to a woman will introduce trouble into your life and ministry. This is probably why Jesus did not marry. He allowed women to minister to Him, but He did not marry any of them.

But and if thou marry, thou hast not sinned; and if a virgin marry, she hath not sinned. Nevertheless such SHALL HAVE TROUBLE IN THE FLESH: but I spare you.

1 Corinthians 7:28

12. THE DISQUALIFICATION OF BISHOPS: Bishops are tested for their ability to stay with one woman. Marriage to one woman brings about the first test that a bishop has to overcome in order to rule the church. Failure to overcome the challenges posed in your life through marriage will disqualify you from being a leader in the house of the Lord.

A bishop then must be blameless, THE HUSBAND OF ONE WIFE, vigilant, sober, of good behaviour, given to hospitality, apt to teach;

1 Timothy 3:2

CHAPTER 7

Warning: Some People Are Married to Devils

Even so must their WIVES be grave, NOT SLANDERERS (DIABOLOS), sober, faithful in all things.

1 Timothy 3:11

In the scripture above, Paul warns wives not to be *"diabolos"*. What is *"diabolos"*? *Diabolos* is the devil. The devil is one of the names for satan. What are the other names of satan? What are the titles of satan? Satan's titles are well known - THE TEMPTER, THE ACCUSER, THE OPPOSER, THE ADVERSARY, THE DECEIVER, THE MURDERER and THE DESTROYER. These names and titles of satan can be used in place of *"diabolos"*, in the scripture above and can be applied to wives.

When a pastor or deacon's wife becomes a devil, she becomes an adversary, an opposer, an accuser, a tempter, a liar and a murderer.

There are many people who would describe their wives as the greatest deception of their lives because after marriage, they found that their wives were not who they thought they were. Outsiders are deceived by the beauty and charm of the deceptive wife. (Marriage to a deceiver).

There are many people who would describe their wives as the greatest temptation in their lives. The temptation to commit adultery, to divorce, to be angry, to be frustrated, to be defeated are real in many marriages. (Marriage to a tempter).

There are many people who would describe their wives as the greatest adversary in their lives. There are people who recognize their wives as their greatest opposition. (Marriage to an adversary).

There are many people who would describe their wives as the greatest accuser in their lives. Sadly, some wives have taken up the job of accusing their husbands. (Marriage to an accuser).

There are many people who could describe their wives as the greatest destruction to their lives and ministries. There are people who feel that their lives have been destroyed because of their marriages. (Marriage to a destroyer).

There are people who would describe their wives as the reason for their stress, illness and eventual death. (Marriage to a murderer).

Anyone who is married to an opposer, an accuser, a tempter and a liar is experiencing what it means to be married to a devil.

Why would I say such terrible things? Why would I use such strong words? These are not my words. These are the words found in the Bible.

Is the devil a destroyer? Yes, he is a thief and a destroyer (John 10:10).

Is the devil an opposer? Yes, he is an opposer (1 Peter 5:8).

Is the devil an accuser? Yes, he is an accuser (Revelation 12:10)

Is the devil a tempter? Yes, he is a tempter (Matthew 4:3)

Is the devil a liar and a murderer? Yes, he is a liar and a murderer (John 8:44).

If you are a pastor's wife, make sure that you are not an opposer.

If you are a pastor's wife, make sure that you are not an accuser.

If you are a pastor's wife, make sure that you are not a deceiver.

If you are a pastor's wife, make sure that you are not a temptation.

If you are a pastor's wife, make sure that you are not a destroyer.

If you are a pastor's wife, make sure that you are not a devil.

If you are a pastor's wife, make sure that you do not cause the death of your husband.

If you are any of these things to your husband, you are a devil to your husband!

Many great men of God have experienced terrible things at the hands of their powerful wives. When John Wesley was seventy-five years old, he wrote his very last letter to his wife Molly and said,

"IF YOU WERE TO LIVE A THOUSAND YEARS, YOU COULD NOT UNDO THE MISCHIEF YOU HAVE DONE."

John Wesley

This is an amazing message from a man of God to his wife. **"If you were to live a thousand years, you could not undo the mischief you have done."** John Wesley did not intend his letter to his wife to become public. As usual, men of God try to give a good PDA (Public Display of Affection) to outsiders. Although women look angelic, they are clearly not angels. They are beset with weaknesses, sins, problems and failings just as men are.

Many ministers are spiritual, committed and driven men. Many times, they are married to women who are weaker and less committed to God. Many women are weak and do not have the physical and emotional strength needed to withstand the storms of life and ministry.

Even so must their WIVES be grave, NOT SLANDERERS *(DIABOLOS)*, sober, faithful in all things.

1 Timothy 3:11

Indeed, women are not angels and Apostle Paul actually warned wives not to be a *"diabolos"*, a word which is translated to mean a "devil".

The word *"diabolos"*

The word, *"diabolos"* is usually translated into the word "devil" and refers to the literal devil. The word *"diabolos"* is used thirty-eight times in the entire New Testament.

Thirty-five times, the word *"diabolos"* is translated into the word devil. For instance, "And Jesus was led into the wilderness to be tempted of the devil (*'diabolos'*)." That word "devil" is translated from the word *"diabolos"*. (Matthew 4:1)

Three times, the word *"diabolos"* is used to refer to human beings. (Acts 13:10, 1 John 3:8, 1 John 3:10)

On one occasion, the word *"diabolos"* was used to describe Judas. Jesus said, "Have I not chosen you, and one of you is a devil (*diabolos*)." (John 6:70)

On two other occasions, the word *"diabolos"* is used in a warning to Bishops' and to deacons' wives. I can understand that the translator did not have the boldness to translate the word *"diabolos"* into "devil" as he had done thirty-five times before. In any case, whether he translated the word *"diabolos"* as "devil" or not, it still means "devil". (1 Timothy 3:11, Titus 2:3)

1. Paul warned pastors' wives not to be devils.

Even so must their WIVES be grave, NOT SLANDERERS (*DIABOLOS*), sober, faithful in all things.

1 Timothy 3:11

This scripture should have read:

"Even so must their WIVES be grave, NOT DEVILS, sober, faithful in all things."

1 Timothy 3:11

"Pastors and deacons" wives can turn into devils! That is why Paul warned pastors' wives not to turn into devils. Deacons' wives are warned not to turn into "diabolos".

Why would Paul warn pastors' wives not to turn into devils? Because a pastor's wife can become a strong accuser of her husband. A pastor's wife can also become a strong opposer to her husband. Through accusations and opposition, some women are transformed into literal human devils that their husbands have to contend with.

Not all pastors have good marriages! Some have really great marriages. Some have good and nice marriages. Some have average marriages and some have terrible marriages. Adoniram Judson was called "three times lucky" because he married three times and each marriage was good.

There are many men of God who are dealing with tangible, physical female devils in their homes. Some of them would tell you that the greatest opposition and challenge to their lives and ministry are the women they are married to.

2. Paul warned older women not to be devils.

> But speak thou the things which become sound doctrine: that the aged men be sober, grave, temperate, sound in faith, in charity, in patience. THE AGED WOMEN likewise, that they be in behaviour as becometh holiness, not false accusers (***DIABOLOS***), not given to much wine, teachers of good things;
>
> Titus 2:1-3

This scripture should have read:

> "But speak thou the things which become sound doctrine: that the aged men be sober, grave, temperate, sound in faith, in charity, in patience. THE AGED WOMEN likewise, that they be in behaviour as becometh holiness, NOT DEVILS, not given to much wine, teachers of good things;"
>
> Titus 2:1-3

Older women can also turn into *"diabolos"* and behave just like the devil. Older women are susceptible to turning into devils. Many ministers have wives who are not as nice as they were when they were younger. Some of these older wives have turned into devils with time.

I did not write the Bible. Neither do I want to re-write it. Let's read it together and accept what we see. The scripture clearly says that these older women can become false accusers, which is *"diabolos"*.

Why is that? Many older women are disappointed, disillusioned and disheartened about life. You will notice that younger women are generally more sweet, cheerful, happy, peaceful, flowing and nice. You will also notice that some older women are more stern, snappy, strict, unsympathetic and irritable. Disappointments of life may have opened the door to devils of bitterness in older women.

It is Wrong to Glorify a *"Diabolos"*

Because women are angelic and weak looking, they often attract support and sympathy instead of the rebukes that they need! Badly behaved wives must be rebuked and corrected. It is wrong to glorify a *"diabolos"*! It is wrong to magnify a *"diabolos"*! It is wrong to encourage a *"diabolos"*! It is inappropriate to give a *"diabolos"* more authority!

Many women do not have the spiritual strength to resist the devil. They must be counselled and controlled. It is wrong to elevate a *"diabolos"* pastor's wife to even greater positions of authority.

CHAPTER 8

Warning: Beware of the Error of Elevating Wives

For three things THE EARTH IS DISQUIETED, and for four which it cannot bear: For a servant when he reigneth; and a fool when he is filled with meat; For AN ODIOUS WOMAN WHEN SHE IS MARRIED; and an handmaid that is heir to her mistress.

Proverbs 30:21-23

The error of elevating wives beyond the biblical prescription is contributing to divorce, confusion and conflict in the church. It is the error of crowning a "Queen of Confusion" (QOC).

One pastor of a massive church lamented to me, after his wife divorced him, "I elevated my wife and made us co-partners, co-founders and co-pastors. That is why she challenged me and fought me so much. She wrote books and sold them in the bookshop. She was an author, and so was I! She was a pastor, and so was I! She was a speaker, and so was I! We seemed to be equal and that was my greatest mistake. She was the most unsubmissive and pretentious creature you could ever imagine." How sad!

Scriptures about marriage seem to lower and suppress women, giving them a very low position in relation to men. Generally speaking, the scriptures do not make husbands and wives equal in the marriage. I also do not know of any scriptures that make pastors and the pastor's wife equal in ministry. Yet, modern Christians love to present pastors and their wives as co-founders, co-partners, co-pastors, co-leaders, co-authors, co-speakers and co-directors.

Why is it that modern Christians disregard these scriptures? Why do modern Christians act as though the Bible is mistaken in what it said about women? Why is this? Is it right?

Apostle Paul was very strong about controlling the women in our midst. It is the only issue on which he challenges all who claim to be prophets or spiritual. He challenges them to acknowledge that women are supposed to be quiet and in subjection. Indeed, it is when women are in subjection that they are happiest. Nasty, quarrelling and discontented women are actually unhappy as they fight to be what they are not.

Let your WOMEN KEEP SILENCE in the churches: for it is not permitted unto them to speak; but they are commanded to be under obedience, as also saith the

law. And if they will learn any thing, let them ask their husbands at home: for it is a shame for women to speak in the church.

What? Came the word of God out from you? Or came it unto you only? IF ANY MAN THINK HIMSELF TO BE A PROPHET, OR SPIRITUAL, LET HIM ACKNOWLEDGE THAT THE THINGS THAT I WRITE UNTO YOU ARE THE COMMANDMENTS OF THE LORD.

1 Corinthians 14:34-37

Why does the Bible say the woman is to be silent and in subjection? It is to avoid the mistake of crowning and elevating a *"Poor Performer"*, a *"Wild Cat"*, a *"Jezebel"*, a *"Quarrelsome Queen"* and giving her great power. It is to avoid the giving of a seat of authority and power to such a wicked person.

The model of ideal and equal partnership of couples in ministry is not the Bible picture. It is nice to see these equal partnerships, but you do not see this picture of equal couples in the Bible.

Why should a woman who does not look after her own children be crowned and empowered? Why should a woman who charges her husband a fee for having sex be elevated and empowered? Why should a Jezebel be glorified and enthroned in the church? Why should an accuser be honoured and lifted up in the midst of the congregation?

To empower and glorify a fool is to disturb the world with confusion! Placing inappropriate people on a throne of glory is to disquiet the earth. The reason why your ministry is so small is because you are "wiser than God". No one is more righteous than the Word of God. You will only live to confirm its validity. You will live to confirm that the Bible is true.

CHAPTER 9

Warning: There is a Woman in the Basket

Then the angel who was speaking to me came forward and said to me, "Look up and see what this is that is appearing."

I asked, "What is it?"

He replied, "It is a measuring BASKET." And he added, "This is the iniquity of the people throughout the land."

Then the cover of lead was raised, and THERE IN THE BASKET SAT A WOMAN!

He said, "THIS IS WICKEDNESS," and he pushed her back into the basket and pushed the lead cover down over its mouth.

Zechariah 5:5-8 (NIV)

This is a prophetic book. It is a book that speaks prophetically about women and their marriages to ministers of the gospel. Marriage brings out the true, and often surprising, behaviour of Christian women. A prophetic revelation is an uncovering of hidden realities so that there can be light and deliverance for God's people.

The scripture above shows an interesting vision from the prophet Zechariah. He saw a basket before him and asked the angel, "What is this?"

The basket represented the iniquity of the people in the land. But there was more to come. The basket had a lid. And when the lid was removed, behold, there was a woman in the basket!

This vision shows that there is a basket with a surprise woman in it. This vision shows how a woman can be a surprise to you. This book is a revelation about the women that are hiding in the basket, ready to be revealed in your life. The woman who will come into your life is in a covered basket. She may be the greatest surprise of your life!

When the woman in the basket was uncovered, the angel exclaimed to Zechariah; *"This is wickedness"!* In other words, wickedness would be manifested by and through this woman. This is wickedness! What a shock! What kind of wickedness is this? It is the surprise wickedness that would come to Zechariah and to the world through the woman.

The angel quickly slammed the lid shut to contain the wickedness in the basket. He wanted to prevent the wickedness in the basket from coming out. The wickedness in the basket was the woman. Don't forget the statement, *"This is wickedness"*.

Many pastors have been surprised by what was in their basket. Just as Zechariah was shocked when a woman came out of the basket, they are surprised that a woman or a wife could be the source of problems. There are many who can say that the greatest problem of their lives is the marriage they are in. Many pastors who do not do well have difficult marriages.

Instead of the angel saying, "This is a nice person," or, "This is a gift to you," he said, *"This is wickedness"*!

The angel could have said, "This is the greatest blessing of your life." He could have said, "This is something precious that will make you happy." But he did not! He said, *"This is wickedness"*! The woman you see in the basket will be the instrument of wickedness against you!

In this book, we are going to learn about the different surprises that men of God have experienced from the basket. For some of them, the most appropriate exclamation has been, *"This is wickedness"*!

Perhaps, within your basket is a *Perfect Pretender* or a *Silent Beauty*. Some people open their basket and find a *"Wild Cat"*, a *"Jezebel"* or a *"Poor Performer"*. This is wickedness! Other ministers have been shocked to discover a *"Quarrelsome Queen"* within their basket.

There are pastors who feel ashamed to describe *The Unmotivated Asexual* personality they have married. Perhaps, the greatest surprise in the basket is the *"Quarrelsome Queen"* and the *"Unyielding Opposer"*, because the woman they met in church was once so pleasant and so caring. This is wickedness!

Indeed, it must have been a surprise when the basket yielded no other than a woman who was a *"Prison Officer"* as well. Who would have ever thought of getting married to a *"Prison Officer"*? This is wickedness! In the basket was the one who would keep them in a virtual prison for the rest of their lives.

There are still more surprises to come from this basket of wickedness. A divorce-prone beauty can rise out of the basket to send you to the divorce courts at one point or another of your life. Little did you know that the woman you were getting married to was not capable of submitting to a man!

I can only imagine the shock that some men have had when they discovered that they were actually married to a mental patient. "My wife is depressed, anxious and irritable. My home is an unofficial mental institution. There is no peace and it does not make sense because there should be a lot of peace."

It is sad to hear the lamentations of some husbands as they describe the *Uncaring Independent* woman they have. And what of the "*Loveless Oldie*"? She is the surprise who will rise out of the basket in her middle age!

It is time to believe that the vision of Zechariah's basket is a reality. It is time to be ready for the surprises that lay in wait for men of God. It is time to be ready to combat the wickedness that is hidden in the basket of life.

The Spirit of Cleopatra

One day, I had a surprising revelation. Whilst counselling a stubborn, "unchanging" wife to love her husband and be nice to him, I heard a voice saying, *"It is Cleopatra. It is Cleopatra."* I was amazed because the Lord was showing me the spirit I was dealing with. I was dealing with *"the spirit of Cleopatra"*.

Indeed, some men open their basket of marriage and find in it the spirit of Cleopatra. What on earth is the spirit of Cleopatra? I researched a bit and found out many amazing things about the spirit of Cleopatra.

The spirit of Cleopatra comes to draw you, to seduce you, only to rear up in pride like a cobra. Everyone has seen a picture of a rearing cobra that lifts itself up in readiness to strike.

Why does a cobra rear up in pride? A cobra rears up to oppose you, to attack you, to bite you, to accuse you and to destroy you. The spirit of Cleopatra is an evil spirit that possesses some women and makes them rear up in pride to oppose you. Through the spirit of Cleopatra, your career and ministry can be brought to an end.

Cleopatra is famous for being brought to Caesar rolled up in a rug. When the rug was rolled out, there was beautiful Cleopatra. Cleopatra then proceeded to seduce and charm Caesar. The sign of Cleopatra is called the *"Uraeus"*. The *"Uraeus"*, Cleopatra's symbol, is the sign of the rearing cobra!

A woman with the spirit of Cleopatra is brought to you nicely wrapped and beautifully presented! It is because of the beautiful presentation of this person that you are attracted, captured and seduced in the first place.

After you are married, you will see the cobra rear itself. When the cobra rears itself, it is your time to experience the pride, the opposition, the accusations and the sharp bite from a woman. People who are married to the spirit of Cleopatra experience a proud woman full of opposition, unending reasons, arguments, accusations and fault-finding. The spirit of Cleopatra will sting you and end your ministry. May you be delivered from the evil spirit of Cleopatra from today!

SECTION 2:

TYPES OF MARRIAGES

CHAPTER 10

Why Pastors Paint a Picture of Perfection

If any man come to me, and hate not his father, and mother, and wife, and children, and brethren, and sisters, yea, and his own life also, he cannot be my disciple. And whosoever doth not bear his cross, and come after me, cannot be my disciple.

Luke 14:26-27

Many ministers love to paint the picture of perfection.

Jesus Christ did not in any way paint a picture of perfection for those who would serve Him. He promised tribulation, difficulty and great challenges to those who would follow Him. He even predicted family problems when He said, "If any man come to me, and hate not his father, and mother, and wife, and children, and brethren, and sisters, yea, and his own life also, he cannot be my disciple" (Luke 14:26).

Jesus meant there would be real trouble and real challenges for people who were called to His service. Nothing is going to be perfect because you are serving God!

Pastors, like politicians, seek to give a perfect picture of their lives and marriages. It is as though ministers of the gospel are standing for election and need to present the picture of a super successful marriage to the public. Because of this need to present pictures of perfection, most people do not present the true state of their lives. This is why the announcement of divorce of several great men of God comes as such a shock to so many. A perfect picture is painted for so long and then it all comes crashing down!

Jesus said, "I receive not honour from men" (John 5:41). He did not need to have the respect of men as do many ministers of the gospel today. We seem to need the approval of the masses. Jesus actually said that some people would have great marital difficulties including hating their own wives because of the ministry.

If any man come to me, and HATE not his father, and mother, and WIFE, and children, and brethren, and sisters, yea, and his own life also, he cannot be my disciple.

Luke 14:26

Apostle Paul was very clear when he said you would have trouble when you got married (1 Corinthians 7:38). He was not ambiguous about this at all. This does not mean Apostle Paul was a bad person. You would hardly hear a minister of God say there is trouble in his marriage today. Meanwhile, there is a lot of trouble in a lot of ministry marriages.

Some people say things like, "I have never quarrelled with my wife before."

They say things like, "My wife is an angel sent from heaven."

Others say, "If marks were given for marriages, I would get 100%."

Still others say, "I don't know how to live without my wife. I would be totally lost in this life if my wife was not with me."

Others say, "We sleep in each others arms every day."

Some say, "My whole life revolves around reading books and having my wife around me. With these two things, I am the happiest person in this world."

Others say, "My life was not complete until this refining influence came to me." `

I have heard all these statements before and they came from wonderful men of God who had wonderful marriages. However, there are a number of difficulties that arise from these descriptions.

1. This perfect picture can be misleading because everyone has a different way of describing things. There are people with even better marriages who would not use these descriptions and would not describe their marriages in such a way. There are people with even better marriages who would describe their marriages as 60% perfect. There are also those with poor marriages who would describe their marriages as being 100% perfect.

2. This perfect picture can also be misleading because children of picture-perfect-marriages can receive an erroneous picture of marriage. In Billy Graham's book "*Nearing Home: Life, Faith and Finishing Well*," his daughter described her confusion when she got married. She felt

the challenges she was experiencing in her marriage were unusual. She thought she was experiencing an aberration of what was normal. Billy Graham describes how he and his wife hid any misunderstandings they had in their marriage from their children. The children never suspected that there were any misunderstandings. The children only saw a perfect picture. Such children can go away confused and even leave their perfectly normal marriages because it does not seem to be as perfect as they expected.

3. The perfect picture of marriage can be misleading to men of God who do not have perfect or good marriages. Many have average marriages! Some have terrible marriages. Others have wonderful experiences. Just as in every sphere of life, the bell diagram is true. Most people are in the middle and most people are average. The perfect picture presented by some ministers confuses young ministers about their experiences in marriage. Some ministers feel like divorcing because they want to have the 100% experience of marriage. They do not know that most people have the 50%.

4. There are different categories of marriage. Some people are getting hundred per cent in their Category 1 marriage. Others are getting a hundred per cent in a Category 3 marriage. A hundred per cent in Class three is different from a hundred per cent in the final year of university.

I think the picture that Jesus painted is more real. The picture presented to us by Jesus is more realistic. It contains predictions of tribulation, trouble, division and great persecution. That is the true picture! Dear pastor, do not be confused by the apparent perfect marriages that some people seem to have. You are probably an average pastor with an average life! However, you may also be experiencing one of the extremes. Through this book, you will receive understanding, knowledge and wisdom, which will stabilize your life.

Through the word of God, you will be able to stabilize and strengthen your life. You will gain wisdom that will help you build your life, your ministry and your marriage.

"Through wisdom is an house builded; ...

Proverbs 24:3

God is building up your family, your life and your ministry. The devil is intent on tearing down your life and breaking up your family. It is only through practical wisdom and knowing how to apply knowledge, that you can build a happy life.

When you understand how something happens, you have gained understanding. When you have understanding, *you become more stable,* not easily pushed to and fro.

... by understanding it is established:

Proverbs 24:3

By understanding many things, you will be stabilised in your mind about life, marriage and ministry. There are many things that can destabilise you or unsettle you in marriage. Through the understanding you are getting in this book, you will become more established in your marriage.

The metamorphosis of your spouse into a different person from the one you knew before you married, is one of the greatest trials you will ever experience. All the changing scenes of life can work against you and destroy your ministry. *Always remember that understanding establishes you.*

There are many problems that do not have solutions. I cannot deceive you. Many marriages will never improve, no matter what you read or do. You are just supposed to go through and pass your test of life, marriage and ministry. *The good news is that, with a deeper understanding, your marriage will be established.*

Knowledge makes a man strong.

A wise man is strong; yea, a man of knowledge increaseth strength.

Proverbs 24:5

Through the knowledge you will gain in this book, you will increase in strength to fight the good fight of faith in the ministry. Instead of being weakened by your marriage, God will strengthen you to fight on! This strength will come through the knowledge you will gain from the Word of God.

CHAPTER 11

Category 1, Category 2, Category 3 Marriages

But in a great house there are not only vessels of GOLD and of SILVER, but also of WOOD and of EARTH; and some to honour, and some to dishonour.

2 Timothy 2:20

There are three categories of marriage:

Category 1 marriages

Category 2 marriages and

Category 3 marriages

After you read this chapter, you can decide which category of marriage you are experiencing. To help you understand the categories of marriages, you must also understand the categories of illnesses that exist. Illnesses exist in three categories too.

Category 1 Illnesses, Category 2 Illnesses and Category 3 Illnesses

Common malaria is a Category 1 illness. Cancer is a Category 2 illness. An illness that is threatening to kill you is a Category 3 illness. You are experiencing a Category 3 illness when you are near death.

Remember that, Malaria, a Category 1 illness, can also progress and kill you. Cancer, a Category 2 illness can also progress and kill you. But cancer, a Category 2 illness is far more likely to kill you than a Category 1 illness, although there are many people who do not die from their cancers. An illness is considered Category 3 when it threatens your life. You may have cancer but your life is not under threat.

As you can see, you are in danger when you have a Category 2 illness. Obviously, you are in much more danger when you have a Category 2 illness than when you have a Category 1 illness. It is also not surprising to see someone with a Category 2 illness soon progress into a Category 3 situation.

Category 1 Marriages, Category 2 Marriages and Category 3 Marriages

A Category 1 marriage has problems that do not normally threaten the existence of the marriage.

Category 2 marriages have serious problems that are likely to threaten the existence of the marriage.

Category 3 marriages are marriages that are on the brink of breaking up.

CATEGORY 1 MARRIAGES

In this kind of marriage, there are no serious spiritual, moral or physical deficiencies in either partner.

A Category 1 marriage is what I call the normal marriage between committed Christians. This normal marriage has certain problems and difficulties that are common to almost every marriage. They are the problems that occur because men are so different from women.

In this type of marriage there is no serious defect in either partner. The couple has problems that you hear of with almost every couple. Below is a list of some possible problems or complaints that a Category 1 marriage may have.

Category 1 Marriage Problems

1. My husband does not talk much.

2. My husband does not remember birthdays.

3. My husband does not remember anniversaries.

4. My wife does not remember anniversaries.

5. My wife is too hard.

6. My husband does not help with the housework and cooking.

7. My wife never initiates sex.

8. My husband does not bath or dress the children.

9. My husband does not take me out for dinner.

10. My husband does not like going shopping with me.

11. My husband wants to have sex even when I am tired from working the whole day.

12. My wife does not like cooking.

13. My wife cannot cook like my mother.

14. My husband wants to eat certain foods that I do not know how to make.

15. My husband gives more money to his parents than to my parents.

16. My wife does not flow with my mother.

17. My wife does not get along with my sisters.

18. My wife is rude.

19. My wife is always quarrelling with the house helps.

20. My wife talks too much.

21. My wife is always shouting at the children and the maids.

22. My wife does not care for me when I am sick.

23. My wife does not massage me.

24. The food is never ready when I get home.

25. My husband comes home too late.

26. My husband is always on his computer.

27. My husband talks more to the church members than he talks to me.

28. My wife does not have exciting sex.

29. My wife is more interested in the children than she is in me.

30. My wife is always on the phone.

31. My husband is always out with his friends.

32. My wife only cooks when there are visitors.

33. My wife is stubborn.

34. My wife does not listen to me.

35. My husband does not listen to me.

36. My wife is quarrelsome.

37. My wife is not spiritual.

38. My husband is not spiritual.

39. My husband does not have his quiet time.

40. My husband does not pay tithes.

41. My husband is too slow.

42. My wife is too slow.

43. My wife falls asleep when we are watching a film.

44. My husband does not help with the homework.

45. My husband always wants to have sex.

46. My husband does not give me enough money.

47. My husband does not contribute to the house-keeping.

I am sure you can add to this list of problems. This list of problems will be found in many Category 1 marriages. The list does not vary much because human beings are the same everywhere.

Many ministers who have a Category 1 marriage are grateful to God for the good marriage they have. A Category 1 marriage is the best kind of marriage that exists. Many pastors who have a Category 1 marriage have the delusion that something better exists elsewhere. What they do not know is that there is usually something worse that they have been delivered from.

One day, I met a pastor who had Category 1 problems. He had no idea what it was like to have Category 2 problems. After many years of marriage, his wife deteriorated and he began to have Category 2 problems. It was only then that he appreciated the fact that he had enjoyed a Category 1 marriage for many years. He began to wish for his old problems to come back and for the new ones to disappear. He wanted his marriage to revert to a Category 1 marriage!

CATEGORY 2 MARRIAGES

Category 2 marriages are a different story. In this type of marriage, one of the spouses has a defect or a deficiency that can threaten the marriage itself. In a Category 2 marriage, a serious moral defect, a serious personality defect or a serious spiritual defect exists in one of the partners.

Some ministers have Category 1 marriages and some have Category 2. It is common for a minister with a Category 1 marriage to fail to understand the life and problems of a minister with a Category 2 marriage.

People who have Category 1 marriages often criticize Category 2 marriages and think that those with Category 2 marriages are not doing something right. They say things like, "Follow the seven steps to a perfect marriage and you will not have any of these problems. Love your wife and you will have a perfect marriage."

Category 2 Marriage Problems

1. **Where one of the partners has sex outside the marriage you have a Category 2 problem.** This is very complicated because having sex outside the marriage in today's world is dangerous. A faithful partner can develop a sexually transmitted disease through no fault of theirs. If your partner has sex with outsiders, you are in danger of acquiring a life-threatening disease. When one of the partners has sex outside the marriage, he has introduced a life-threatening problem to the marriage.

   I remember a couple in which one party was having constant affairs outside. They were both pastors and they agreed to use condoms at home so that they could continue to live together. The spouse was simply unable to guarantee that he would not have an affair with someone else. These two pastors continued to live together in this way in the face of a problem that genuinely threatened their marriage's existence.

2. **Where a wife openly challenges and opposes her husband, you have a Category 2 problem.** In the ministry, it is important to be able to lead your wife around. If you have lost the ability to lead her, how can you lead the congregation? If God tells you to go somewhere, you will not be able to go there because your wife will not follow you.

A great man of God was sent on a mission by a Mission Agency. When he excitedly told his wife about the new mission, she said to him flatly, "I am not going anywhere."

She continued, "I am soon to be promoted in my work place, where I will be made a Principal Officer. I will not leave and I will not go with you. Besides all this, I have diabetes and I don't see how it can be treated on the mission field."

After some weeks, she realised that her husband had been greatly affected by her refusal to go to the mission field. So she said to him, "I am giving you the permission to marry another person. When I married you, I said I would follow you anywhere. But now I will not go and so I release you from our marital vows. Please feel free to take another girl and marry her."

Obviously, this forty-year-old pastor and father of three children could not marry anybody else. As a devoted husband, he could not bring himself to do any such thing. His lot was to endure the solitude, the loneliness and the temptations, alone on the mission field.

3. **Where a wife constantly accuses her husband, you have a Category 2 problem.** Where a husband constantly accuses his wife, you have a Category 2 problem. This is the type of marriage that John Wesley experienced. The

violent and openly challenging woman is difficult to deal with and control. What usually happens with this kind of marriage is that many people who witness the behaviour of this violent accusing woman, sympathise with the pastor. They recognise that the pastor is labouring with a monster by his side.

Constant accusation, whether violent or soft-spoken make it impossible for the partners to love each other. This even happens in politics where politicians who constantly accuse each other of terrible crimes cannot and do not love each other. When they do get into power, they imprison each other because they hate each other.

A marriage to a soft-spoken accuser is a Category 2 marriage. This defect is a serious problem and it threatens the marriage. Soft-spoken accusations create a very tense situation in the home, and the home is destroyed through the accusations. The home of such couples can be likened to a place where adultery has taken place. There are constant upheavals, arguments, accusations, counter-accusations and defences.

Unfortunately, the pastor who has married a soft-spoken accuser receives sympathy from no one. No one can imagine that he is experiencing the same things as happens in the violent, openly challenging and accusing woman's marriage. He therefore constantly hears people praising his wife and praying to have a marriage just like his.

4. **Where a wife is a mentally ill person, you have a Category 2 problem.** Mental illness ranges from psychological conditions to depression and schizophrenia. Princess Diana was suspected of having a borderline personality disorder. Some women have the mental condition called depression. Others have split personalities. Some have what is called a bipolar disorder whilst others have a delusional disorder. Indeed, marriage to a mentally ill person is a Category 2 marriage with life-threatening problems.

CATEGORY 3 MARRIAGES

A Category 3 marriage is one that is on the brink of separation or divorce. This type of marriage may appear normal on the outside but there is a real threat of separation or divorce. The home swings from periods of apparent peace to periods of serious tension, bordering on separation. It is quite like having tropical rainstorms interspersed with bright sunny days.

One day, I heard the announcement that a great man of God was getting divorced.

When I heard the news I sunk into depression because I felt that pastors' marriages were under severe attack. One day, however, I had the opportunity of travelling abroad and meeting up with a close friend of this man of God who had just announced his divorce.

I eagerly discussed this new divorce situation and asked him, "Is it not possible for this marriage to be restored?"

He said, "No, I don't think so."

I asked again, "Are you really sure that it is not possible for this great pastor's marriage to be restored?"

He stared at me blankly. Then he muttered under his breath; "I am surprised that they have even lasted up to this point. I have been expecting them to break up for years. They almost separated many times. I am surprised that they are still together."

I realised that this man of God had been in a Category 3 marriage for years. It was a marriage that had been under a constant threat of dissolution. After some more investigation, I found out that the pastor's wife had often shown signs of a mental illness.

Category 3 Marriage problems

In Category 3 marriages, there is constant talk of divorce and separation. You will hear statements like, "I can't take it anymore!"

"It's too much!"

"I am going back to my mother!"

"Even my father never treated me this way!"

"I am going back to my father!"

"I will drive you out of this house!"

"You are the cause of all the problems in our marriage!"

"It's over!"

"I have suffered in silence for too long!"

"Everybody must know what is happening in this house!"

Some ministers with a Category 1 marriage can metamorphose directly into a Category 3 marriage. This is because any problem can grow or be magnified until a Category 3 situation develops. People with a Category 2 marriage more easily progress into a Category 3 marriage.

Once a Category 3 marriage is established, the union of the couple is threatened and the possibility of separation and divorce is real.

Both Category 1 and Category 2 marriages can shift down to a Category 3 type of marriage. Men of God who are determined to remain married and have Category 1 marriages rarely descend into Category 3. However, you will find many shallow Christians with Category 1 problems opting for divorce.

Men of God who really love their wives, but have Category 2 problems, are often forced down into Category 3 marriages. Many of the divorces of famous pastors you hear about are pastors who have been in Category 2 for a long time. They had Category 2 problems that became Category 3.

Be careful not to criticise pastors with Category 2 and 3 marriages.

Many pastors who have Category 1 marriages do not understand the constant tension, quarrels and upheavals that characterize pastors with Category 2 and 3 marriages. They often criticise and despise pastors who get divorced. They secretly think to themselves, "This pastor is fallen. He is done for! I am sure he is in love with some lady in the church. He is not principled! He is not holy!"

I have watched ministers with Category 1 marriages criticise ministers with troubled marriages. I have heard pastors with Category 1 marriages condemn pastors with Category 2 and 3 marriages. Be careful! As you criticise others, you are revealing your ignorance about the categories of marriage. Pray hard that your nice Category 1 marriage does not turn into a Category 2 or 3 marriage!

CHAPTER 12

The Devoted Husband (A1)

> Then Joseph her husband, being A JUST MAN, and not willing to make her a public example, was minded to put her away PRIVILY.
>
> **Matthew 1:19**

We must define the term "devoted husband" (A1 husband) as it has been used in this book. A devoted husband is a husband like Joseph. Even though Joseph seemed to have been greatly wronged by his Mary's mysterious pregnancy, he would not let anyone know about it. "He was minded to put her away privily!"

A devoted (A1) husband suffers privately and secretly in his marriage without telling anyone. People would not usually know when he is experiencing challenges and unpleasant things in his marriage. The Bible calls him a just man who was not willing to make a bad example of his wife.

A "devoted (A1) husband" is an ideal husband. He is a model husband that many women would only dream of having. What kind of characteristics do such husbands have?

1. A devoted (A1) husband is a spiritual person.

2. A devoted (A1) husband wants to be in the ministry.

3. A devoted husband (A1) is a moralist with very high ideals of morality.

4. A devoted (A1) husband has a deep-seated vision of having a very successful marriage.

5. A devoted (A1) husband is someone who will never think of divorcing his wife.

6. A devoted (A1) husband is someone who has many ideals and dreams about how his family and home should be.

7. A devoted (A1) husband is someone who says wonderful things about his wife.

8. A devoted husband (A1) never reports any negative or evil that he experiences in his marriage.

9. A devoted (A1) husband gives a good picture about marriage all the time.

10. A devoted (A1) husband respects his wife and treats her with great dignity.

11. A devoted (A1) husband is a husband who is loving and caring.

12. A devoted (A1) husband is a husband who treats his wife as a partner.

13. A devoted (A1) husband is a husband who wants to do everything with his wife and go everywhere with his wife.

14. A devoted (A1) husband is a husband who loves family times of togetherness and likes to take lots of pictures.

15. A devoted (A1) husband is a husband who is romantic and loves romantic scenes and times with his wife.

16. A devoted (A1) husband is someone who calls his wife often to find out where she is, how she is, what she is doing and if she is ok.

17. A devoted (A1) husband is someone who goes shopping for the family.

18. A devoted (A1) husband is someone you do not have to ask for money.

19. A devoted (A1) husband is someone who helps his wife with the house duties and chores.

20. A devoted (A1) husband is someone who is completely open to his wife about what he has and what he is doing.

21. A devoted (A1) husband is someone who buys gifts for his wife.

22. A devoted (A1) husband is someone who takes his wife out for lunches and dinners.

23. A devoted (A1) husband is someone who wants to be with his wife alone.

24. A devoted (A1) husband is someone who always appears in public with his wife. He says, "We" instead of "I" and always mentions his wife.

25. A devoted (A1) husband is someone who has no other potential females lurking around him.

26. A devoted (A1) husband is someone who gets married as early as he can.

27. A devoted (A1) husband is someone who is focused on his wife and sees her as the source of all pleasure that he may ever have in this life.

28. A devoted (A1) husband is someone who loves the parents and family of his wife and treats them the same as his own family.

29. A devoted (A1) husband is someone who has an ideal number of children.

30. A devoted (A1) husband is someone who takes his children to school.

31. A devoted (A1) husband is someone who lies in the arms of his wife to sleep every night.

32. A devoted (A1) husband is someone who sleeps in the same room and bed with his wife.

33. A devoted (A1) husband is someone who understands his wife and any weaknesses she may have.

34. A devoted (A1) husband is someone who does not condemn his wife when she is at fault.

35. A devoted (A1) husband is someone who builds a house for his family.

36. A devoted (A1) husband is someone who is quick to apologise when he sees that he is wrong in anything.

37. A devoted (A1) husband is someone who is kind to his wife.

38. A devoted (A1) husband is someone who leaves love notes and communicates frequently about his love.

39. A devoted (A1) husband is someone who tells his wife, "I love you" several times a day.

40. A devoted (A1) husband is someone who tells his wife "I love you more than you love me."

41. A devoted (A1) husband is someone who notices his wife's dressing and compliments her. He says, "You are looking nice. I like your hair. You are very beautiful."

42. A devoted (A1) husband is someone who cares for his wife when she is not well and nurses her tenderly until she is well.

43. A devoted (A1) husband is someone who is there when his wife is having a baby.

44. A devoted (A1) husband is someone who buys many nice things, like clothes, for his wife.

45. A devoted (A1) husband is someone who buys all his wife's underwear.

46. A devoted (A1) husband is someone who takes his family for holidays.

47. A devoted (A1) husband is someone who cooks sometimes for the family.

48. A devoted (A1) husband is someone who serves breakfast to his wife in bed.

49. A devoted (A1) husband is someone who organises pleasant surprises for his wife. He organises surprise birthday parties, birthday cake, birthday cards and birthday flowers for his wonderful wife.

50. A devoted (A1) husband is someone who goes shopping with his wife or allows her to go shopping.

51. A devoted (A1) husband is someone who takes his wife to do her hair and waits for her.

52. A devoted (A1) husband is someone who goes everywhere with his wife.

53. A devoted (A1) husband is someone who wants to use the same towel as his wife.

54. A devoted (A1) husband is someone who wants to eat together with his wife from the same plate and drink from the same glass as his wife.

55. A devoted (A1) husband is someone who wants to use the same toothbrush as his wife.

56. A devoted (A1) husband is someone who does not need a special day or a special occasion to celebrate his wife. He buys presents and organises celebrations on any day.

57. A devoted (A1) husband is someone who is very understanding about his wife's sexual needs, and does not demand much sex from her.

58. A devoted (A1) husband is someone who always gives a good report about his wife.

59. A devoted (A1) husband is someone who wants to give a public display of affection so that the whole world will know that he has an excellent marriage.

60. A devoted (A1) husband is someone who grieves when his wife is dead and does not marry for a long time to preserve her memory and to prove to everyone that he truly loved her. A devoted husband struggles to recover from the loss of his wife. A devoted husband may not marry again when his wife dies. A devoted (A1) husband will prove to everyone that it is difficult to replace his wife.

CHAPTER 13

The "Fend for Yourself" Husband (X5)

But if any provide not for his own, and specially for those of his own house, he hath denied the faith, and is worse than an infidel.

1 Timothy 5:8

U nfortunately, devoted (A1) husbands are not so common. A "fend-for-yourself" (X5) husband is the opposite of a devoted (A1) husband. Christian ladies struggle when they are married to "fend-for-yourself" (X5) husbands. There are many Christians who are "fend-for-yourself" husbands.

Marriage to a "fend-for-yourself" (X5) husband is no easy experience. Marriage to such a person is an adventure in self-provision, fending for oneself, building houses and becoming a multi-tasking "Tarzan" woman. Women who are married to a "fend-for-yourself" (X5) husband have a completely different experience from those who are married to the devoted (A1) husband.

Characteristics of a "Fend-for-yourself" husband

1. A "fend-for-yourself" (X5) husband is a husband who is not spiritual and does not direct his family into spiritual things.

2. A "fend-for-yourself" (X5) husband is a husband who does not go to church much. You must fend for yourself.

3. A "fend-for-yourself" (X5) husband is a husband who is lazy. You must fend for yourself.

4. A "fend-for-yourself" (X5) husband does not remember marriage anniversaries and does not celebrate them.

5. A "fend-for-yourself" (X5) husband is a husband who is selfish and self-centred. You must fend for yourself.

6. A "fend-for-yourself" (X5) husband is a husband who expects a lot but has little to offer. You must fend for yourself.

7. A "fend-for-yourself" (X5) husband is a husband who has no time for anything concerning the marriage. You must fend for yourself.

8. A "fend-for-yourself" (X5) husband is a husband who does not help with any of the housework and domestic chores. You must fend for yourself.

9. A "fend-for-yourself" (X5) husband will not pay or organise for any of the domestic chores to be done to help his wife. You must fend for yourself.

10. A "fend-for-yourself" (X5) husband is a husband who will not lift a finger to look after the children. You must fend for yourself.

11. A "fend-for-yourself" (X5) husband is a husband who does not have kind words or love for his wife. You must find love from wherever.

12. A "fend-for-yourself" (X5) husband is a husband who is comfortable with the fact that he does not provide for his family. You must find your own provision.

13. A "fend-for-yourself" (X5) husband is a husband who does not discuss anything with his wife.

14. A "fend-for-yourself" (X5) husband is a husband who hides his finances from his wife. You must find your own finances.

15. A "fend-for-yourself" (X5) husband is a husband who does not look after the children. You must look after them yourself.

16. A "fend-for-yourself" (X5) husband is a husband who does not pay his children's school fees. You must fend for yourself and your children.

17. A "fend-for-yourself" (X5) husband is a husband who does not talk or chat to his wife. You must talk to yourself.

18. A "fend-for-yourself" (X5) husband is someone who does not have sex with his wife. You must fend for yourself if you want to.

19. A "fend-for-yourself" (X5) husband is a husband who does not talk about his wife. Someone else must talk about you.

20. A "fend-for-yourself" (X5) husband is a husband who does not take his wife out for dinner. Find your own dinner.

21. A "fend-for-yourself" (X5) husband is a husband who does not show any concern for his wife. You must care for yourself.

22. A "fend-for-yourself" (X5) husband is a husband who does not build a house for his family. Build your own house.

23. A "fend-for-yourself" (X5) husband is a husband who is not faithful to his wife.

24. A "fend-for-yourself" (X5) husband is a husband who is a bad example for his children to follow. Find a better example for your children.

25. A "fend-for-yourself" (X5) husband is a husband who gets used to his wife moving around and catering for all the needs that come up in the family.

26. A "fend-for-yourself" (X5) husband is a husband who expects his wife to take care of him.

27. A "fend-for-yourself" (X5) husband is a husband who does not pay the house bills for the home. You must fend for yourself.

28. A "fend-for-yourself" (X5) husband is a husband who does not buy any clothes for his wife. Buy your own clothes.

SECTION 3:

THE BEASTS OF MARRIAGE

CHAPTER 14

Stages of Deterioration of Nice Marriages

In the morning it flourisheth, and groweth up; in the evening it is cut down, and withereth.

Psalms 90:6

1. STAGE 1: *FME* STAGE

FME stands for FAMILIARITY MINUS EXCITEMENT

Many marriages start with excitement, love, romance, joy and admiration. After the initial excitement of being married to the great, devoted man of God, familiarity sets in. There is nothing so great any more about being married to this "great man of God". There is nothing so great about being told "I love you" ten times a day! There is nothing so great about receiving love notes. They are even boring! There is nothing so great about having all your needs met. There is nothing so great about being taken out for dinner every week. There is nothing so great about being together and having sex often. As a result of familiarity, wonderful things like receiving breakfast in bed, having your husband cook for you, having your husband show concern, lose their significance.

The lack of honour and awe reduces excitement to almost zero. Devoted husbands struggle with trying to create excitement in their marriage. Indeed, some devoted husbands find it difficult to achieve erections with their uninterested and familiar wives.

Many devoted husbands actively seek to encourage their wives to generate excitement in sexual things. Devoted husbands try hard to convince their wives about the importance of being exciting, delightful, sexual beings as they were in the days of their youth. Several devoted pastors give up on sex after having several fruitless meetings about sexual excitement and the sexual act.

2. STAGE 2: *POO* STAGE

POO stands for PRIDE and OPPOSITION ORIENTATION

A girl in love is oriented towards supporting the man she loves. When there is deterioration of the relationship, the person who was oriented towards supporting is now oriented towards opposing, resisting and arguing. Pride makes you argumentative. Pride makes you resistant to your spouse. The danger in getting married, and especially getting into a second marriage lies in the probability of POO.

POO is the possibility that the spouse becomes the opposer to all that the husband is trying to do. Before marriage, there will be the greatest flow between the man and the woman. She seems to understand everything and agrees. She is oriented towards flowing, assisting and helping. But when deterioration sets in, she becomes more oriented towards opposing and disagreeing with everything that is suggested.

Watch carefully and you will see how many women are actually their husbands' greatest opposition. Such devoted husbands will publicly introduce wives as their greatest help, but actually their wives are their greatest hindrance. Opposition is a manifestation of pride. Pride makes you believe that you are as good as the other person. Pride makes you argue.

Many wives are the greatest opposers to all the ideas of their husbands. If the idea comes from elsewhere they will take it. If it comes from their own husbands they will frown on it. Before the marriage, she was probably the greatest supporter. Before marriage, she would see him as a wise man full of the anointing and wisdom. But with deterioration, she becomes the *Unyielding Opposer*.

During the stage of POO, she will never say "Yes"! She will never agree! She will never yield! She will never accept that she is wrong! She will never be soft! She will never obey!

Ask careful questions and you will discover that many wives do not obey their husbands any longer. They do not even believe in the wisdom of their husbands. Indeed, POO is a dangerous swerve from the flowing, yielding, happy and energetic young bride that you once had.

3. STAGE 3: *GAP* STAGE

GAP stands for GRUDGING AVERAGE PERFORMANCES

A Grudging Average Performance is what many devoted pastors receive when the awe of being married to the man of God dies down. There may be sexual intercourse, but it happens grudgingly and not excitedly.

The lady who used to kiss her husband, initiate sex, adopt exciting styles, move excitedly and vigorously during the sexual act, moan, groan and gasp in pleasure, is now a virtual dead body. She lies there like a cadaver, as the man single-handedly strives on to ejaculate into his unimpressed and uninterested wife. Indeed, the GAP has appeared and has probably come to stay.

I once asked a lady who was giving Grudging Average Performances to her husband to do the same things she did with her previous numerous boyfriends.

I asked. "Who were your boyfriends in the past? Whom did you sleep with in the olden days?"

"Other people's husbands" she answered. "Every single person I slept with was already married."

"Do you perform the same energetic and exciting manoeuvres as you did with your boyfriends?" I asked.

She smiled and said, "Of course not. No, I don't."

"What kind of things were you doing with these married men?"

She smiled sweetly, "Of course kissing, sweet smiles, exciting styles, oral sex, active movements, groaning, moaning, gasping with vigorous classical orgasms!" Wow!

Somehow, this lady had managed to marry a devoted "A1" husband. She knew in her heart that this devoted "A1" husband

95

would never leave her until she died. The kind of man she had was the everlasting, faithful, "I-will-never-leave-you" kind of person. Because of that, she supplied him with Grudging Average Performances. The men who did not marry her but only gave her a little money had received all her exciting, energetic, acrobatic, gymnastic and romantic sexual performances.

The devoted "A1" husband who had married her did not benefit from her sexual skills. She was too tired to give such performances to this faithful, everlastingly devoted husband. He apparently did not "deserve" such performances. He would only receive Grudging Average Performances (GAP).

4. STAGE 4: *ROL* STAGE

ROL stands for RECEIVER OF LITTLE

Unfortunately, many devoted husbands move into the stage of ROL. ROL means a "Receiver of Little". In the ROL stage, you will notice that the husband actually receives little from the marriage. After he has provided his name, his ring and his sperms for children, he begins to receive little. ROL is now in full force. The wedding pictures are placed in the living room for all to see and admire.

The devoted husband realises that he has only been used as a profile booster for his wife, a sperm donor for children and a make-me-important puppet for the public.

He has successfully lifted up his wife's image in society by making her into a well-recognised Madam. Unfortunately, he may never be served at home, never receive any love, never receive any attention or ever receive any care. His sexual needs may not be provided for at all. If they are, he will receive a GAP (Grudging Average Performance).

The devoted "A1" man's need for excitement as he gets older is never provided. Some wives of devoted husbands travel away and live in different countries for many years. They visit their husbands once a year, knowing that he cannot and will never be unfaithful to her. Of course, such devoted husbands never say anything bad about their wives. They calmly take it in and quietly mention to people that their wives are out of town.

Many devoted husbands have muttered in their quiet moments "I now understand why Mr X (an unbeliever) had many external affairs with so many young girls." Many unbelievers have no time to become a Receiver of Little (ROL). Many unbelievers will not accept Grudging Average Performances (GAP). They will not stand for that. Unbelievers will go out of their houses to receive the comfort, the softness, the delights, the love, the attention, the interest, the food, the sex, the conversation, the company and the niceness that they need.

Many devoted "A1" husbands, because they are unwilling to have affairs, stay at home *without* softness, *without* sexual delights, *without* any love, *without* any kindness, *without* anyone showing attention, *without* being served food, *without* exciting sex and even *without* any conversation at all.

5. STAGE 5: *RC* STAGE

RC stands for RESPONSIBILITY CONTRACTOR

The stage of being a "Responsibility Contractor" is when the devoted husband realises that he actually receives nothing from the marriage he has entered into. He has basically put himself forth to have and to own certain responsibilities. At this stage, he realises that he is there to be a sperm donor, to look after the children, to pay their school fees, to get a house for everyone and to get nothing in return.

This is especially manifest in an older pastor who marries a younger lady who already has children. He becomes a responsibility contractor in charge of her small children, her mother, her father, her cousins, her sisters and all that concerns her life.

6. STAGE 6: *NCP* STAGE

NCP stands for NEGATIVITY of CONTINUOUS PRESENCE

In addition to the woes that come from GAPs, ROLs and RCs, NCPs also set in. Some women are very negative in their presence. How is this possible? Their presence invokes quarrels, accusations, contention, debate, anger, confusion, tension and unhappiness. Imagine that! After being a Receiver of Little (ROL), experiencing Grudging Average Performances (GAPs) becoming a Responsibility Contractor (RC) and losing all excitement through familiarity, you now have to endure the negativity of the person's presence.

The "Negativity of Continuous Presence" speaks of the negative effect of having somebody who is always around. The negativity of this continuous presence is manifested when you are unable to pray or be spiritual because of the continuous presence of a spouse.

There are many devoted husbands who are grateful when their wives travel away. Each trip is a relief from the negativity of the continuous presence of this woman. It is often not a problem for such pastors to be separated from their spouses for long periods. After all, they are Responsibility Contractors and there is no excitement but only responsibilities.

7. STAGE 7: *HRD* STAGE

HRD stands for HEIGHTENED REBOUND DEPRESSION

There is usually depression and sadness when people want to get married but have no one to marry. This sadness is heightened when a brother actually marries but ends up as a Receiver of Little. Some husbands suffer a lot from rebound depression because they receive little.

Second marriages can have "Heightened Rebound Depression". People marrying a second time have many delusions. The mere sight of their new wife turns them on and flashes of excitement pass through their spine. They develop dreamy eyes and imagine floating away on pink clouds of ecstasy.

Unfortunately, this is often not the case. The person who is coming along to be the bride has no intention of fulfilling such dreams. She has her own mind of having a child and receiving the financial security she needs. Her mind is on how her social status in life will improve by the marriage. Soon enough, the devoted husband becomes a Receiver of Little (ROL) and a Responsibility Contractor (RC). These realities can lead to a return of the sadness that was there before marriage. Indeed, husbands of *"Loveless Oldies"* (see Chapter 24) suffer greatly from Heightened Rebound Depression.

CHAPTER 15

What it Means to be Married to a *Perfect Pretender*

Let love be WITHOUT DISSIMULATION. Abhor that which is evil; cleave to that which is good.

Romans 12:9

Many people are truly artificial. There is no way to know who they really are or what they are really like. A newly married man once sent a message from his honeymoon chamber. It was short, but revealing. The message said, "It seems I got the wrong one!" Many people are shocked at who they really married.

Love without dissimulation is loving someone without any pretence! Marriage to the Perfect Pretender is a journey of discovery. Today, many ladies have false hair, false eyebrows, false nails, false eye lashes, false hips, false breasts and false body shapes. The skin of the Perfect Pretender is not as smooth as it looks. All these false things create a large pool of Perfect Pretenders in every church.

The pretending beauty is an inviting, charming, sweet, delightful, enjoyable, agreeable and exotic beauty that draws and excites. The pretending version that is perfectly charming, delicious, exotic, appealing, charismatic and pleasant is presented to the public.

The new husband, on the other hand, will have to discover the "reality version" at home. He will be made to discover the real temperament and disposition of his beautiful bride. The unsuspecting young man will find out that many things about this person are not real.

It is not easy to pretend for long

"I want to be myself! Let me be free!" No one can maintain an artificial presentation of beauty, perfection and gentleness for long. Many decide in their hearts to "become themselves" at home. "Let me be myself!"

The natural self is not propped up, is not bathed, is not polite, does not always act sweet and gentle. Many women are not naturally perfect, beautiful or gentle. In "being themselves", these ladies go through a rapid deterioration from the picture they presented.

The Temperament is Uncovered

Perfect Pretenders do not easily reveal their true temperament. However, the one who marries her will discover everything for himself.

He may discover that his Perfect Pretender is a choleric woman. Choleric women are quick to take decisions, so they quickly recognise the power they have over their husbands. Soon, you may have a sharp, angry, strict, decision-taker in charge of affairs at home.

He may discover that his Perfect Pretender is a phlegmatic woman. Phlegmatic temperaments will descend into laziness, placidity and lack of expression.

He may discover that his Perfect Pretender is a sanguineous woman. The sanguineous wives will allow their homes to turn into a chaotic, completely mixed up, jumbled up and topsy-turvy environment. These very sanguineous women will appear beautiful, charming, jolly, friendly and huggable when they step out of the home.

He may discover that his Perfect Pretender is a melancholic woman. The beautiful melancholic that you married will turn into a silent, moody, keep-to-myself personality. There will be no sound in the house as she arranges and re-arranges the same things over and over again. One brother lamented, "My wife sweeps behind me as I walk through the house."

The Spirituality is Uncovered

You may now discover that the spirituality of the wife is not as deep as it seemed. Most pastors are far more spiritual than their wives. People assume that anyone who lives in the pastor's house must be spiritual. But this is not always the case. The Perfect Pretender was simply looking for a man to marry. She was not looking for ministry. She would have been equally happy marrying a bank manager if he had been available.

The Lack of Submission is Uncovered

Perhaps the greatest discovery will be when he finds out that his wife is not as submissive as she looks. All beautiful women look so submissive. But submission can vanish within a few weeks of marriage. When pastors' wives no longer submit to their husbands, they lose their spiritual covering. Because they are no longer under a covering they are spiritually naked and evil spirits have direct access to them.

Some wives of pastors are seriously afflicted by demons because of their pride and refusal to submit. Evil spirits love to take on women directly, avoiding their covering. When women are not humble, they do not acknowledge that they need a covering. They proceed without a real spiritual covering and experience direct fellowship with evil spirits and entities.

These evil spirits then make the women more hardened and unyielding. Soon, the beauty is turned into a real beast in the hand of evil spirits. The beauty may then be used to accuse, oppose and fight the man of God.

There are many men of God who would tell you that their greatest problem in ministry is their wives. Their wives are not the sweet, soft and gentle ladies that they first seemed to be.

Laziness is Uncovered

Many pastors are amazed when they discover the laziness hidden within their Perfect Pretender. Because marriage involves so much hard work, the Perfect Pretender is unprepared to work hard for the marriage to be a success. Once she has her wedding ring, her marital name and the prestige of being married to the man of God, she becomes very lazy and refuses to do the hard work that is necessary to make a marriage happy.

All her energy and efforts are directed at dressing nicely to show off and continue her life of pretence. At home, her husband is on a journey of discovery of the real person. He discovers that she has no energy to bath once she arrives home in the evening!

There is no energy to brush her teeth in time to be kissed! There is no energy to wash herself clean of sweat, urine and other dirt. On the outside, everyone praises her beautiful hairstyle and her nice perfume. The unfortunate brother who married this Perfect Pretender is on his journey to discover many unpleasant smells.

Demons are Uncovered

A Perfect Pretender is always a candidate for demon infestations. Demons love to hide under the cloak of pretence. All kinds of evil spirits are uncovered in a marriage to a Perfect Pretender. Sometimes, it is difficult to imagine the demons that exist behind a beautiful face.

Hurts and Wounds are Uncovered

A jolly and smiling girl may now reveal that she is actually easily hurt and easily upset. Unforgiveness and bitterness reveal a hard, unyielding and strict headmistress personality. This uncaring, hard and unyielding woman is a far cry from the soft, caring and sensitive bride she seemed to be. Indeed, our young "A1" husband is completely taken aback by what he has discovered after marrying a Perfect Pretender.

CHAPTER 16

What it Means to be Married to *A Silent Beauty*

...Will you keep SILENT AND PUNISH US beyond measure?

Isaiah 64:12 (NIV)

The "*Silent Beauty*" is a beautiful lady who comes into your life but has little to say or to offer in terms of conversation. Her beauty is her best asset because that is what attracts the unsuspecting young man to her. Most of the things that are in her heart are not said. She keeps many things within her. The *Silent Beauty* is someone who never had many real friends. She is not relational and may comment that no one ever proposed to her apart from her husband.

Throughout her relationship, her main and only friend is her husband. She waits for him and depends on him for all forms of human interaction.

1. People who are silent are carefully holding back themselves from relating to others.

    For a long time I have kept silent, I have been QUIET AND HELD MYSELF BACK…
    Isaiah 42:14 (NIV)

2. A person who does not speak when she should, punishes those who live around her. It is not a nice experience to live in the presence of a silent non-communicative beauty. The environment around a silent and moody person is a controlled and manipulated environment. When the person cheers up, everybody is allowed to cheer up too.

    …Will you keep SILENT AND PUNISH US beyond measure?
    Isaiah 64:12 (NIV)

3. Relating with a silent person is the same as relating with the dead. Your home can be called the realm of the dead when you are married to a *Silent Beauty*.

    Let me not be put to shame Lord, for I have cried unto you; but let the wicked be put to shame and BE SILENT IN THE REALM OF THE DEAD.
    Psalm 31:17 (NIV)

4. A person who speaks and chats creates a refreshing atmosphere around her. It is always nice to be in the presence of a friendly, chatty, conversation creator.

    I will speak, THAT I MAY BE REFRESHED: I will open my lips and answer.

    Job 32:20

5. A person who is silent has a heart full of things that she is not saying. It is unsettling to be with a person whose heart is full of things that she is not saying.

    ... for out of the abundance of the heart the mouth speaketh.

    Matthew 12:34

The Beast

After she is married, you will find that the *Silent Beauty* only relates to her husband. She does not make or have any friends in the church. Hardly any lady in the church can be called her friend. A lot of texts and mails may be sent to her but she does not respond to these texts or relate to many people.

When her husband comes home she has little to say to him. She claims that he is the one who talks. She is flat and bland in her speech with little to contribute and little to say. The pastor may be distressed because he wishes that his wife would engage the congregation and chat with the members.

Indeed, people who are acquainted with her may consider her to be a friendly person because she is a specialist at social pleasantries such as, "Hello", "How are you?" "How are the children?", "How is your wife?" Her conversations never run any deeper than these initial pleasantries. The compliments of the season are what you can expect because our *Silent Beauty* has very few deep relationships!

In the ministry, a *Silent Beauty* is of little value. She will not speak to the church members and she will not wait around in church. She has nothing to say to anyone. She does not engage the members in deep conversation and deep friendship. You could easily say to the *Silent Beauty* the same words that John Wesley said to his wife:

IF YOU WERE BURIED JUST NOW, OR IF YOU HAD NEVER LIVED, WHAT LOSS WOULD IT BE TO THE CAUSE OF GOD?

John Wesley

At home, our *Silent Beauty* is also unemotional and inexpressive. There is no emotion, no feeling and no sensation that flows out of her towards her husband. All feelings seem to be within her as she silently and unemotionally relates with him.

Sexual relations for our flat, bland and *Silent Beauty* consist mainly of allowing her body to be used as a receptacle of her husband's male organ. She has nothing to say or do. She has nothing to offer and few feelings to express. She considers sex as something that he is doing to her. She simply waits for it to end!

After church she waits silently for her husband to finish talking to his numerous fans. She sits silently alone, waiting in the car, placing him under tremendous psychological pressure to finish his meetings quickly and come on home.

The Dangers

1. Flatness: The man of God complains about a lack of life and enthusiasm in his *Silent Beauty*. He looks out of his window and sees other vivacious, cheerful and friendly girls who relate with the congregation happily. Oh, how he wishes he had chosen one of those lively gems! What a difference it would have made in his life!

2. External friendships: Her husband may be driven to chat with and befriend other people who would meet his needs for fellowship, happiness and interaction.

3. Intimidation: Through her silent and psychological manipulation, she intimidates her husband all the time. She puts her husband under a lot of pressure by making him feel uneasy with her silence. She silently makes him cut down his interaction with others and limits his ministry.

CHAPTER 17

What it Means to be Married to *A Wild Cat*

It is better to dwell in the wilderness, than with a contentious and an angry woman.

Proverbs 21:19

A *Wild Cat* wife is an untrained, unspiritual and disobedient woman. She is one of the most difficult personalities to live with. This kind of wife is the worst kind of uncontrollable creature a pastor would like to encounter. She lives for herself and seems not to have any boundaries of common sense, love, decency, restraint, caution or spirituality.

The Beast: Disrespect

Such a woman will insult her husband in the presence of any one. I know wives who criticise their husbands and tear them down in front of their children. A *Wild Cat* wife of a man of God was known to shout at her husband in the presence of the children. She would call her husband names and say, "You are a bush man! You are nothing! I will show the world that you are not a man of God! Idiot! Idiot! Idiot!"

Such a woman would try to win the hearts of the children to her side through her negative depiction of her husband. Unfortunately, this often backfires and the children often end up gravitating towards their father and away from their mother.

The Beast: Violence

Some of these *Wild Cat* ladies are known to hit their husbands. I have known some of them to repeatedly attack their husbands in front of their children. No one would believe that such a beautiful and charming lady would physically attack her husband.

Then the cover of lead was raised, and there in the basket sat a woman!

He said, "This is wickedness," and he pushed her back into the basket and pushed the lead cover down over its mouth.

Zechariah 5:7-8 (NIV)

111

I remember a *Wild Cat* that warned her husband to speak up and answer all questions that she asked. When the pastor refused to answer her questions, she tore up her marriage certificate in front of him. As he fought with her to save a piece of his marriage certificate, she promptly put the rest of the certificate in her mouth and taunted him by chewing it up in front of him.

Such marriages are dangerous because it is uncertain as to what harm the *Wild Cat* may do to her husband.

One husband woke up in the morning to find a knife stuck by the bed. He was startled and asked, "What is this knife for?" When she told him what she was planning to use the knife for, he could not believe his ears. Trembling and shaking, he called his senior pastor and told him, "I am in great danger in my own house."

A husband once came with his wife for counselling. The pastor noticed some marks on his head and asked, "What happened to you?"

It transpired that he had been hit several times by his wife who had thrown a chair at him. Even though he was the same size as his wife, he seemed to be genuinely afraid to fight back.

One day, a pastor married a beautiful and gentle-looking lady. This lady metamorphosed into a fighting, challenging opposer. She would even hit and punch her husband when she had the opportunity. She would also attack people in the church. This unfortunate pastor had to move from room to room in his house to avoid the lady he had married as he tried to live peacefully in the same building with her. It is amazing that gentle and beautiful ladies can metamorphose into this kind of beast.

One Sunday, after delivering a powerful sermon, the pastor went home to enjoy the Sunday afternoon. This couple had no children. After lunch there was a discussion that turned into an argument. Known to be violent, the wife attacked her husband when she could not stand what he was saying.

Her husband made a dash for his car to escape. However, before he could get into his car, this beautiful pastor's wife ran out to the car park and slashed his tyres with all her strength deflating them. The pastor was unable to make his getaway by car so he escaped from the house on foot. He disappeared into the bushes and was not seen for many days. Indeed, he had to escape for his very life's sake from a beautiful but knife-wielding, tyre-slashing woman! The next Sunday, the pastor preached powerfully in church, but no one had any idea that he had been on the run during the week, escaping for his dear life's sake.

Some husbands are so filled with the scripture "husbands love your wives" that they ignore basic standards of safety and common sense. God has no intention of destroying you through your spouse. Marriage was intended to provide help for your life. Marriage was not intended to destroy you.

The Beast: Bad Motherhood

Instead of being a good example to the children, such a woman is a bad mother to her children. She is full of resistance and arguments and every nice family event is in danger of turning into a huge quarrel. A man married to such a woman has to be both a father and a mother to his children.

A young man told me how he had cared for his pastor's children for several years because his pastor's wife had no time for her own children.

"What was she doing?" I asked, "Why couldn't she look after her own children?"

"I don't know" he answered. "All my pastor's children were looked after by people like myself because his wife was simply non-performing in the real sense of the word."

The Beast: Public Embarrassment

John Wesley's wife was known to attack him openly. She once attacked him in front of his other pastors whilst he was having lunch in a canteen. She would attack him and accuse him of consorting with other women. This wild woman embarrassed John Wesley time and time again.

According to one of Methodism's travelling preachers: "Once when I was in the north of Ireland, I went into a room and found Mrs Wesley foaming with fury. John Wesley was on the floor, where she had been trailing him by the hair of his head. She herself was still holding in her hand venerable locks, which she had plucked up by the roots." Allegedly, this took place about a year and a half after they married.

On another occasion, John Wesley was at a meeting with more than sixty of his Methodist ministers. A lady called Sarah Ryan was serving the pastors with food. Mrs Wesley burst into the room shouting and waving her finger at Sarah. Then she said, "The whore now serving you has three husbands living."

A pastor's child once told me how their father would give them instructions and their mother would intentionally go against the instructions. The father would say, "Do not watch television", but the mother would put on the television for the children to watch.

The father would say, "You must not buy food from the street", and the mother would buy the very food that their father had said they should not have.

Husbands are embarrassed as their *Wild Cat* wives publicly oppose them on every little instruction. The home becomes the ground for a ding-dong battle between husband and wife with the children at the centre of it all.

The Beast: Pretence

Central to the survival of this *Wild Cat* wife is a glorious image and public sympathy. The *Wild Cat* loves to bask in the glory of her position. The *Wild Cat* loves to receive all the respect and reverence due her position.

The *Wild Cat* is completely driven by the outward impressions that she wants people to have of herself and of her marriage. This hypocrisy is very painful for those who suffer the pain of living with her. To gain public acceptance she may even cry and tell many lies.

Unfortunately, many women are deceived and deceive others too. Many women deceive others with ease. A *Wild Cat* needs these lies to keep up the false image she has built for herself. Fake eyelashes, a fake smooth face without spots, fake breast size, fake hips, fake hair, fake nails and fake pleasantness are the hallmark of such women. Almost everything about them is unreal. That smiling, cheerful-looking girl taking a selfie, may actually be the most depressed, moody and unfriendly person.

The Beast: Disobedience and Unspirituality

Although many women have the title "Reverend Minister" they are often not truly spiritual. Shouting in tongues is not what reveals your spirituality. Obedience to the Word of God is what reveals your love for God.

I remember speaking to one such unspiritual woman who carried the title of "Reverend". I asked her to stop her evil behaviour. I pointed out to her that she was going against the Word of God. She shrugged and continued doing exactly what was against the Word of God.

Years later, when her life was destroyed, she tried to contact me to deliver her from the darkness she had created for herself. Unfortunately, I was not in a position to help her any more. Her husband had moved on!

The Dangers

1. Loss of love: A *Wild Cat* is unable to receive her husband as a man of God. She sees him as someone to fight, someone to oppose and someone to resist. Obviously the man of God will find it difficult to love this "opposition party" and treat her as a delicate object.

2. Violence and danger of imprisonment: A pastor who is married to a *Wild Cat* may be forced into violence himself. He may hit his *Wild Cat* in frustration or in self-defence. Such a pastor is also in danger of having a bad reputation for fighting with his wife and hitting her. The pastor may end up in prison for beating up his *Wild Cat*.

3. Divorce: Often, the earlier years of marriage are filled with hope and the young husband has great faith that a change is possible. However, as the years go by, hope fades and the reality sinks in. The young man realises that there will never be a change. Actually, things are going to get worse! The possibility of divorce will loom bigger everyday.

CHAPTER 18

What it Means to be Married to Jezebel

And **JEZEBEL HIS WIFE SAID** unto him, dost thou now govern the kingdom of Israel? Arise, and eat bread, and let thine heart be merry: **I WILL GIVE THEE THE VINEYARD** of Naboth the Jezreelite.

1 Kings 21:7

Jezebel is the infamous wife of King Ahab. The book of Revelation also makes mention of the "spirit of Jezebel". Apparently, the same spirit operating during the time of Ahab was operating in the days of John. You cannot discount the presence, existence and operation of the spirit of Jezebel in our world today. Jezebel is a spirit that attacks great men of God like Elijah. If you are in the ministry and are destined for greatness, you can expect to encounter a Jezebel somewhere! Jezebel is real!

The beauty you marry can become a Jezebel! There in the basket sat a woman!

"Then the cover of lead was raised, and there in the basket sat a woman! He said, 'This is wickedness', and he pushed her back into the basket and pushed the lead cover down over its mouth". (Zechariah 5:7-8)

Always remember that Jezebel can be defeated if she can be identified.

Jezebel is the spirit that attacked Elijah. Any spirit that attacks Elijah is a spirit that is a specialist at attacking men who carry a great anointing.

It is therefore important that every man of God and also the pastor's wife become aware of this spirit and oppose its activities in the church and the ministry. Remember: Thou shall not suffer that woman Jezebel ... !!!

Notwithstanding I have a few things against thee, BECAUSE THOU SUFFEREST THAT WOMAN JEZEBEL, which calleth herself a prophetess, to teach and to seduce my servants to commit fornication, and to eat things sacrificed unto idols.

Revelation 2:20

Jezebel Today

I once spoke to a broken-hearted assistant pastor. He had been the assistant to his senior pastor for twenty-five years. He had worked closely with his senior pastor and faithfully sacrificed for the ministry. Together they had built a powerful mission with thousands of members.

One day, the senior pastor's wife slapped one of the church members during an argument. The church member lost her temper and organised a group of people to protest against the pastor's wife.

"Enough is enough", they exclaimed. "We have had enough of our senior pastor's wife. We will no longer stand for her nonsense. We want her to go! We don't like her! She is an evil person! She has tormented us since our pastor married her! She quarrels, she accuses, she drives away people, she divides the family and now she has slapped one of us."

Following the uproar, the senior pastor resigned and left the church. The pastoral team was broken up and the church virtually closed down. Everyone went their separate ways. The ministry was effectively terminated by the pastor's wife's attack on a church member.

The broken-hearted senior assistant pastor lamented, "We had been together for twenty-five years. We had a great ministry and a great church. Now we have lost everything."

He continued, "I don't even know what I am going to do with my life from now on. Our church is closed down. Our ministry is over!"

Then I asked him, "How did all this happen? How can an entire ministry be terminated overnight? What has caused all this?"

He answered, "I think we made a great mistake with our pastor's wife. She was clearly a Jezebel and we allowed her to operate freely in the church. We thought we were showing respect to our senior pastor so we never confronted her."

He confided in me, "She divided the church. Many people left the church when she married our pastor. She even drove away the pastor's children who were forced to attend another church."

He continued, "But we strongly believed in loyalty to our senior pastor and never confronted her about all the quarrels and divisions she was causing."

After one and a half hours of talking about the effects of having allowed a Jezebel to freely roam around in the church, we parted company.

I did not know how this faithful assistant was going to come by his next meal and live through the next month. He had lost all that he had built up over twenty-five years.

Nevertheless I have a few things against you, because YOU ALLOW THAT WOMAN JEZEBEL, who calls herself a prophetess, to teach and seduce My servants to commit sexual immorality and eat things sacrificed to idols.

Revelation 2:20 (NKJV)

Many people do not understand the scripture that says, "I have a few things against you *because you allowed that woman Jezebel...*" Jezebel is a dangerous spirit that fights great men of God. It fights them through their wives and other powerful influencing figures. A Jezebel must not be allowed to operate freely in the church.

Through the revelation of this book, you will overcome every kind of Jezebel operating in your life and ministry. Scripture tells us not to allow the woman Jezebel to operate freely. Most pastors are too dignified and self-righteous to confront a pastor's wife or to bring her into order. Many pastors want to maintain good relations with everybody. As a result of that, they will not rebuke and correct wives who are out of order. When you allow a Jezebel to roam freely, you, like Elijah, will be tormented without end. When you allow a Jezebel to go uncorrected, you will lose everything just like Elijah lost everything.

Let's see what happened to Elijah. A careful analysis of many great men of God who walk in high levels of the anointing, like Elijah did, will reveal the pattern that I have described below. The patterns produced by a "Jezebel wife" are unmistakable.

Dangers of Being Married to a Woman With the Spirit of Jezebel

1. A "JEZEBEL WIFE" CAUSES A MAN OF GOD TO BE DISCOURAGED IN MINISTRY.

What is it like to be married to a Jezebel? What are the works of this unique spirit whose specialty is to attack God's leading servants? Through a "Jezebel wife", you will experience a severe attack of discouragement that will make you feel like you have achieved enough in ministry. That is the spirit of Jezebel at work. The spirit of Jezebel made Elijah say, "It is enough. I have done enough. I have done more than enough!" You may wonder - what would make a happy and successful man of God say "I have done enough", "It is enough"?

> **But he himself went a day's journey into the wilderness, and came and sat down under a juniper tree: and he requested for himself that he might die; and said, IT IS ENOUGH; now, O Lord, take away my life; for I am not better than my fathers.**
>
> **1 Kings 19:4**

2. A "JEZEBEL WIFE" CAUSES A MAN OF GOD TO BE DEPRESSED IN MINISTRY.

> **But he himself went a day's journey into the wilderness, and came and sat down under a juniper tree: and he requested for himself that he might die; and said, It is**

**enough; now, O LORD, TAKE AWAY MY LIFE; for I
am not better than my fathers.**

1 Kings 19:4

Elijah wanted to die. His prayer was, "O Lord, take away
my life!" Elijah became suicidal after his greatest achievements
in ministry. You may wonder why a person at the peak of his
ministry would ever want to die.

In the same way, you would also wonder why a great man
of God would consider death as a happy escape from his wife.
Through a "Jezebel wife" you will become depressed and will
want to die. When a person does not mind dying, he is depressed.

If you ever experience severe depression where you want
to die, you are probably dealing with the spirit of Jezebel. The
spirit of Jezebel makes you say, "Let me die". It is depression
that makes a person suicidal. There are many pastors who are
suicidal because of problems at home.

One pastor confided in me. He said, "When I had marital
problems with my wife, I considered killing myself twice."

He continued, "Once, I wanted to throw myself down from a
tall building. The torment, the accusations and the pressure from
my wife were too much for me to handle."

I was amazed as I beheld this great man of God confessing
that he had contemplated suicide twice because of his wife.

3. *A "JEZEBEL WIFE" CAUSES A MAN OF GOD TO CHANGE HIS ASSISTANTS AND FRIENDS.*

**Then Jezebel sent a messenger unto Elijah, saying, So
let the gods do to me, and more also, if I make not thy
life as the life of one of them by to morrow about this
time. And when he saw that, he arose, and went for his
life, and came to Beersheba, which belongeth to Judah,
AND LEFT HIS SERVANT THERE.**

1 Kings 19:2-3

A "Jezebel wife" will cause you to set aside the important people in your life. It is mysterious, but it will happen. Through Elijah's interaction with Jezebel, he became terrified and set aside the servant that had been with him for years. Elijah abandoned his main friend, his great helper and his assistant! You may wonder why a person would separate himself from those who practically help him. Sometimes, men of God are forced to change members of their staff because their wife dislikes them. That is Jezebel in action!

Sometimes men of God are forced to dismiss important people from their lives. The departure of these important people often leads to major changes in their ministry. Often, Jezebel secretly forces the man of God to do away with people she does not like.

It is important for the man of God not to "allow that woman Jezebel" to operate freely. Do not allow the spirit of Jezebel to control you and make you remove important people from your life. You must only take decisions, as you are led by the Spirit. You must not be led by your wife, but by the Holy Spirit!

4. A "JEZEBEL WIFE" CAUSES A MAN OF GOD TO END HIS MINISTRY PREMATURELY.

And the Lord said unto him, Go, return on thy way to the wilderness of Damascus: and when thou comest, anoint Hazael to be king over Syria: And Jehu the son of Nimshi shalt thou anoint to be king over Israel: and ELISHA THE SON OF SHAPHAT OF ABELMEHOLAH SHALT THOU ANOINT TO BE PROPHET IN THY ROOM.

1 Kings 19:15-16

A "Jezebel wife" will cause you to end your ministry prematurely. Elijah abruptly ended his ministry. He handed over the reins of his ministry to Elisha long before he had to. The effect of a "Jezebel wife" is indeed mysterious!

I earlier on shared the testimony of the assistant pastor whose senior pastor's wife slapped a church member. It is interesting to note that this twenty-five year old ministry also came to an abrupt end. A large and successful ministry was closed down suddenly by a woman's behaviour. A major church and ministry was terminated by the wife's behaviour. All the pastors of that great church were scattered. The founder of that church became the laughing stock of all his enemies.

Jezebel is the greatest threat to the ministry of powerful men of God. When a man of God operates at the level of Elijah, he has probably overcome many obstacles and it is only a woman like Jezebel who can influence or detract him from his mission. Notice how Elisha was prematurely brought on the scene to take over the office of Elijah. Elijah's handing over to Elisha is an example of a premature and abrupt end of a ministry.

Elijah handed over his ministry when it was at its very peak! Watch out for these signs when you are looking to spot a Jezebel. There is probably a Jezebel somewhere when there is a premature ending to a ministry.

5. A "JEZEBEL WIFE" MAKES A MAN OF GOD BEHAVE ABNORMALLY.

A "Jezebel wife" will cause her husband to behave abnormally. Watch out for abnormal behaviour in a man of God. You would wonder why Elijah would run away from a woman after fearlessly confronting 400 prophets of Baal. Unusual occurrences and unusual behaviour patterns of men of God are often due to Jezebel spirits.

I once watched a man of God do unusual things. He travelled away from his home. He lived away from his home. He always acted frightened when his wife's name was mentioned. He looked nervous and on edge most of the time. And yet God was using him to do mighty things. I found out much later that he had a fully anointed Jezebel in his bedroom.

On another occasion, I noticed a man of God who was usually gentle and soft-spoken, become extremely irritated and angry for a season. His behaviour seemed completely out of sync with his normal way of doing things. I also found out later that he had a Jezebel in his bedroom. Watch out for unusual behaviour in a man of God. He is probably under pressure from a Jezebel!

And Ahab told Jezebel all that Elijah had done, and withal how he had slain all the prophets with the sword. Then Jezebel sent a messenger unto Elijah, saying, So let the gods do to me, and more also, if I make not thy life as the life of one of them by to morrow about this time. And WHEN HE SAW THAT, HE AROSE, AND WENT FOR HIS LIFE, AND CAME TO BEERSHEBA, WHICH BELONGETH TO JUDAH, AND LEFT HIS SERVANT THERE.

1 Kings 19:1-3

6. A "JEZEBEL WIFE" CAUSES A MAN OF GOD TO WANDER ABOUT IN THE WILDERNESS OF MINISTRY.

But he himself went a day's journey INTO THE WILDERNESS, and came and sat down under a juniper tree: and he requested for himself that he might die; and said, It is enough; now, O Lord, take away my life; for I am not better than my fathers.

1 Kings 19:4

A "Jezebel wife" causes her husband to wander about in the wilderness.

Elijah was displaced and began to move around from place to place. His base had been taken away. There are men of God who are roaming about in the wilderness because of a Jezebel at home.

A man of God wrote about how he kept moving house in order to quench the raging storms at home. He moved several times over a period of years. He had hoped that each move to a new home would bring about a change in the terrible marriage they were experiencing. He described how every move to every new building was an attempt to control the Jezebel in his home.

125

I know another man of God who conveniently lived at a place that was a seven-hour flight away from his wife. He did that in an effort to stay away from his marital home.

I know yet another man of God who abandoned his church for several years and moved to live in another country. Everyone thought he was pioneering a new mission overseas. Unfortunately, it was not missionary work that had made him move abroad. He, like Elijah, was on the run!

John Wesley declared that he might have settled down if he had had a loving, good wife. It is possible that John Wesley kept roaming around and achieving great things for God because he could not go back to a peaceful and happy home.

7. A "JEZEBEL WIFE" CAUSES A MAN OF GOD TO TURN INTO THE EXACT OPPOSITE OF WHAT HE WANTS TO BE.

Arise, go down to meet Ahab king of Israel, which is in Samaria: behold, he is in the vineyard of Naboth, whither he is gone down to possess it. And thou shalt speak unto him, saying, thus saith the Lord, HAST THOU KILLED, AND ALSO TAKEN POSSESSION? And thou shalt speak unto him, saying, Thus saith the Lord, in the place where dogs licked the blood of Naboth shall dogs lick thy blood, even thine.

1 Kings 21:18-19

A "Jezebel wife" causes the man of God to become the exact opposite of what he is.

"Ahab, have you killed somebody?" "Ahab, have you taken possession of land that is not your own?" This was a question Elijah was sent to ask Ahab (1 Kings 21:19). Ahab, did not originally intend to murder Naboth, but only made him several offers for his land. Jezebel turned Ahab into a killer of an innocent man.

Jezebel could have advised Ahab to negotiate more with Naboth about his land. She could have advised him to offer Naboth more money for his land; but Jezebel rather turned Ahab into a murderer! When a man of God becomes the exact opposite of what he set out to be, you must consider the possibility of a "Jezebel wife". There is a power that can turn men of God into the exact opposite of what they set out to become.

Jezebel turned Ahab into a murderer. Ahab was not going to kill Naboth. Ahab had no intentions of killing Naboth. Remember that Ahab actually met Naboth and spoke to him directly.

Ahab did not initially arrest or destroy Naboth. However, when his "Jezebel wife" got involved, Ahab killed Naboth and became a murderer. Today, Ahab is remembered for murdering Naboth; something he never intended to do! Many men of God are bent slowly by their Jezebel wives into becoming the exact opposite of what they want to be.

One day, the Holy Spirit whispered to my heart, "I will show you seven famous men of God who have experienced the power of 'Jezebel wives'. " Each of them has become the exact opposite of what they set out to be. The Lord showed me how many of these great men of God, through the intervention, operation and activities of their wives, had became the exact opposite of what they wanted to be. Most of them had the symptoms of depression, discouragement, abnormal travels and abnormal behaviour I have described above.

I remembered several famous pastors who never intended to be divorced. They had loved their wives and they loved the good image they had in marriage. However, through their wives' behaviours, they are all divorced today.

I remembered two famous pastors who served God with all their hearts. They became Christians in school and lived very straight and moral lives. I know this because I know them personally and I know a lot about their personal lives. Through the pushing and pulling of their wives, both of these pastors ended up in prison. They ended up standing trial and being convicted of crimes they did not really commit. They were insulted, ridiculed and treated as worthless criminals. When they became prisoners, they obviously lost their ministries. Like Elijah, they ended up becoming the exact opposite of what they set out to be through their 'Jezebel wives'.

Then I remembered two more famous men of God who ended up divorcing and re-marrying three times. These men of God were the greatest family men you could ever meet. They loved their families and were committed to the ideals of marriage. But they both ended up divorced and marrying at least three times in total. None of them ever intended to be married three times. Both of these pastors had powerful "Jezebel wives" in their homes.

Yet again, I remembered a pastor who was the most amazing, dedicated and committed missionary you could ever find. He was so dedicated on the mission field that he spent twenty-five years fighting for church growth and church establishment in that country. Through his wife's manoeuvres, he one day abandoned the ministry and fled to his home country.

I was amazed to see him flee. Many difficult crises had happened to him over the years on the mission field; but none of them had been able to make him flee. However, through his "Jezebel wife's" involvement, he left the mission field abruptly and never returned.

Always remember these symptoms of a "Jezebel wife". You will never see a woman with the name, "Jezebel" written on her face. But by the symptoms of a man of God's abnormal behaviour, premature handing over of ministry, dismissing valuable assistants and turning into "exact opposites" you will know that a "Jezebel wife" is at large.

Then the cover of lead was raised, and there in the basket sat a woman! He said, "THIS IS WICKEDNESS," and he pushed her back into the basket and pushed the lead cover down over its mouth.

Zechariah 5:7-8 (NIV)

CHAPTER 19

What it Means to be Married to *A Poor Performer*

Then he which had received the one talent came and said, Lord, I knew thee that thou art an hard man, reaping where thou hast not sown, and gathering where thou hast not strawed:

And I was afraid, and went and hid thy talent in the earth: lo, there thou hast that is thine.

His lord answered and said unto him, Thou wicked and slothful servant, thou knewest that I reap where I sowed not, and gather where I have not strawed: Thou oughtest therefore to have put my money to the exchangers,...

Matthew 25:24-27

Jesus told the famous story of people who were given talents. Some performed well and came back with more talents. But one of them was a *"Poor Performer"*. He came back with very bad results. He performed poorly on his mission. Indeed, some wives are *Poor Performers* like this man who was given one talent. A poor performing wife is a disappointment, to say the least. Much was expected from the one talent given to her. Instead she came back with excuses and accusations.

Poor Performers are powerful accusers and great manufacturers of excuses. Their excuses and counter accusations are the only defences they have for their poor performances.

The Poor Performer is a woman of great promise, greatly admired by the outside world and full of charm and attraction. She presents herself as the beautiful lady who should be everything the pastor has dreamed about and wished for. Unfortunately, this is not to be the case.

> **Go and cry in the ears of Jerusalem, saying, Thus saith the Lord; I remember thee, the kindness of thy youth, the love of thine espousals, when thou wentest after me in the wilderness, in a land that was not sown.**
>
> **Jeremiah 2:2**

Anyone who marries a *Poor Performer* has married a lady who dresses up beautifully and looks nice on the outside, but basically has nothing else to offer. Often, she is a beautifully dressed up but lazy woman who has little energy for anything else apart from giving a good impression.

The Beauty

The Poor Performer is a success in public and all the brothers are left wishing that they had chosen such a charming queen. But the one who actually chooses her is going to be disappointed because she is a *Poor Performer* in the private life of her marriage. She is excellent on the outside but has little to offer on the inside. There is a surprise in the basket.

Then the cover of lead was raised, and *there in the basket sat a woman!* He said, "THIS IS WICKEDNESS," and he pushed her back into the basket and pushed the lead cover down over its mouth.

Zechariah 5:7-8 (NIV)

It takes almost no training for a girl to grow up liking clothes, make-up and all the things that make a girl pretty. Because no training is required for this, *The Poor Performer* comes naturally with the skills to look good. Also, it is natural for ladies to want to give a good impression on the outside. *The Poor Performer* is good at giving a good impression on the outside.

Before the marriage to the man of God, she is exuberant with great promises of the delights she will offer to her husband when they get married.

Before marriage her tasty dressing styles greatly stir up the interest of her husband-to-be. Her charming smile, long beautiful hair and her positive attitude are the epitome of attraction.

Before marriage, she says how greatly she desires to have sex with her husband. These statements greatly excite her husband-to-be, who imagines with excitement what he will experience when he gets married to her.

Before marriage, she speaks positively of the kitchen and of the food she knows how to prepare. When asked about her culinary skills, she tells of the "chicken sauce" that she plans to make for her husband.

The young deluded pastor is drawn like a magnet to this exciting creature. "Were you created or were you specially crafted?" he asks. He assumes that this attractive personality has all the qualities that he will ever need and that her public appearance corresponds to her skills in private life. What a shock is in store for him! There is a surprise in the basket!

131

Spirituality: A Poor Performer

One of the worst ever pastors' wives to be written about was John Wesley's wife. She was described as being "NO MORE THAN CONVENTIONALLY RELIGIOUS".   This is a description of someone who was not deeply religious and obviously unspiritual.

Unspirituality is the foundation for all poorly performing wives. John Wesley's wife was such a bad wife that his brother, Charles Wesley said, after enduring insults and complaints from her, "I MUST PRAY OR SINK INTO A SPIRIT OF REVENGE."

One pastor was greatly disappointed in his wife's spirituality. He had been deceived by her apparent interest in God and the ministry before they got married. He could not understand how she had become uninterested in spiritual things after they got married. I explained to him, "She was never interested in spiritual things. You were deceived by her apparent zeal for God."

There are many people in church today who are not interested in spiritual things, but they want a deceived pastor to choose them and marry them.

An unspiritual and disobedient lady is a candidate to becoming a *Poor Performer* in every area of marriage. It indeed takes spirituality and obedience to the Word to be a good performer in all the necessary areas.

The Work of Ministry: A Poor Performer

Instead of helping in the ministry, *The Poor Performer* is unable to engage the church members and relate to them nicely. *The Poor Performer* is a poor hostess and does not make church members feel at home when they come around. If you thought you were going to be assisted greatly in ministry, you made a big mistake. *The Poor Performer* is not hospitable, cannot cater for people, cannot pray, cannot preach, cannot counsel, cannot work on a computer or perform any other administrative work. *The Poor Performer* cannot even get a job to help with the financial situation at home. A *Poor Performer* is nothing and has nothing to offer! Marrying her is like buying a doll! Beautiful to look at, but unable to do anything!

Hard work: A Poor Performer

The man of God is shocked to find out that his beautiful bride is lazy. She is not as wonderful as she looks in public. At home she will not wake up early and do hard work. Anything that involves hard work like cooking, cleaning and working around the house is neglected.

Engaging in hard work is different from getting dressed, painting your face, putting on make-up and wearing artificial hair! *The Poor Performer* is only good at getting her hair done, getting clothes, getting made-up and looking good for the Sunday show. One husband lamented about how he had to wash his wife's panties because she simply would not wash them. A *Poor Performer* will leave all the work undone.

Food: A Poor Performer

A young lady who is untrained and untutored at home is a perfect candidate for a *Poor Performer*. After some time in the marriage it becomes clear to the man of God that his wife can't cook and won't cook.

I remember a pastor who would go home to a beautiful wife, who simply did not know how to cook. He had to buy cooked food from town and bring it home so he could eat together with his wife and children.

The "chicken sauce", which she had spoken of, was an experimental dish she had once made. It was by no means something that could and would be regularly eaten in the house. *The Poor Performer* had read about various recipes on the internet, but had not actually made any of them!

A man of God once became a well-known visitor in every restaurant within ten miles from his house. There was nothing to eat at home and his poorly performing wife would not rise up to the occasion of feeding him.

Another *Poor Performer* caused her husband to become a chimpanzee. His special meal was bananas and he could eat an entire bunch within a few seconds. His house often lacked food because his wife did not like cooking; so he would fill his stomach with bananas every time he did not have food to eat.

Bringing up Children: A Poor Performer

A *Poor Performer* is also poor at bringing up children. She will not get up to give the children a bath and dress them because it is too much work for her to do. Many children are not brought up by their mothers but by maids, servants and other relatives.

Sometimes, the husband is the nanny and the principal caregiver of his children. Meanwhile, *The Poor Performer* struts around proudly in public, showing off the children that she does not look after!

A senior pastor once told me, "For over thirty years of our marriage, my wife never looked after our children. I had to employ people to bath them, to prepare them for school, to cook for them and to help them with their homework. She simply would not do any of the domestic things that had to do with bringing up children." She was just interested in dressing up and looking good.

Home Appearance: A Poor Performer

In the bedroom, our pretty and exciting creature ties up her hair and hides it in an unevenly shaped synthetic black cloth. This black material creates the most unusual head shape ever seen sitting on top of a rounded head. That is all that is left of the beautiful hairstyle that once attracted the man of God.

Our *Poor Performer* strips herself of all forms of jewellery and now resembles a boy, perhaps even her own brother. She is not interested in bathing and dressing nicely at home, since no one will see that part of her. But the pastoral husband must endure this new and homely look without complaint. If he dares say anything about anything, he will receive a myriad of excuses and perhaps one or two counter accusations.

Love and Comfort: A Poor Performer

She is superficial in her relationships. She has no hugs, no eye contact, no nice words, no kisses and no friendliness for her husband. She never cuddles up to him because she is not that type. The person who seemed to be an exciting creature outside has nothing to say at home. She claims she is the quiet type and does not know what to say in conversation to her husband.

She never sits by him to talk to him. She never notices if he is dressed properly or not. If she is a singer, she never sings to him or for him. If she is a secretary, she never does secretarial work for him. She is a *Poor Performer* at home.

Sex: A Poor Performer

In the bed, the sexual performance is of the poorest kind. She offers him "cadaveric sex" 90% of the time. "Cadaveric sex" is like having sex with a cadaver. Just as you can have bad food, you can have bad sex. *The Poor Performer* is an unwilling partner for 90% of her sexual interaction with her husband. She was interested in sex at the very beginning when she wanted to have a child. When that season passed, her interest in sex ended.

Her lack of spirituality and her stubbornness result in low energy for the sexual act. She soon becomes a mattress upon which her husband may lie if he wants. When she does have sex, she never initiates it!

She will say, "It's up to him to do whatever he wants. My vagina is available, if he wants to go there." She is a cadaver, and you need to see it to believe it. There is no interest, no kissing, no sounds, no movement, no oral sex, no styles, no smiles, no energy. Is it any wonder that the man of God stops having sex altogether?

The man of God is in danger of sexual starvation. *The Poor Performer* is completely uninterested in the sex act and wonders why her pastoral husband makes so much fuss about sex.

The Dangers

1. Resentment: The man of God may begin to resent all the activities of his wife in which she receives public praise and acknowledgement for her graciousness and charm. When people say, "behind every great man is a 'great woman'", it irritates the poor performer's husband. He wants to shout that the statement is not true. "I'm a great man but I do not have a great woman behind me."

2. Domestication of the husband: The man of God is in danger of being domestically overworked, as he may have to cover up for the housekeeping lapses of his poorly performing wife. The man of God will be seen cooking in private, serving himself food, serving others food, bathing children, dressing them up, doing their hair, cleaning the home, organising the laundry, wiping up the mess in the house and tidying up. He will do all these things in secret and present his wife to the world as a virtuous woman. Meanwhile, the reality is that she is a *Poor Performer*.

   One pastor told me that he was in danger of starvation because his wife simply would not provide food for him. He said, "My children do not even ask their mother for food any more. They just come to me directly and say, 'Daddy, we are hungry'".

3. Regret: The man of God may regret his marriage to this beautiful, dressing specialist who does not attract him with her poor performance at home. *The Poor Performer* lumbers around the bedroom, totally unaware and totally uninterested in anything domestic or anything sexual.

And cast ye the unprofitable servant into outer darkness: there shall be weeping and gnashing of teeth.

Matthew 25:30

4. Cynicism: The man of God is in danger of becoming cynical and unimpressed with any beautiful girl he sees walking around in church. He may begin to wrongly think to himself that all beautiful girls are poor performers.

CHAPTER 20

What it Means to Be Married to *An Unmotivated Asexual*

... open to me, my sister, my love, my dove, my undefiled: for my head is filled with dew, and my locks with the drops of the night.

Song of Solomon 5:2

Whaat does it mean to be married to *"The Unmotivated Asexual"*? To be married to an *Unmotivated Asexual* is to marry a sexual disappointment. You will always be crying *"Open to me, my sister, my love, my dove, my undefiled: for my head is filled with dew"*. You will always be explaining the importance of sex to your lover. To be married to *The Unmotivated Asexual*, is to be married to someone you will always be begging for sex with pleadings and teachings about its importance. You will always be saying, "Please be kind to me". In the Bible, sex is called "due benevolence". Benevolence, as you know, means kindness.

> Let the husband render unto the wife DUE BENEVOLENCE: and likewise also the wife unto the husband.
>
> 1 Corinthians 7:3

Unfortunately, many people experience wickedness from their wife, instead of kindness.

> Then the cover of lead was raised, and THERE IN THE BASKET SAT A WOMAN! He said, "THIS IS WICKEDNESS," and he pushed her back into the basket and pushed the lead cover down over its mouth
>
> Zechariah 5:7-8 (NIV)

Asymmetry means no symmetry. Azospermia means no sperms. Anaemia means no blood. Asexual therefore means non-sexual. Any woman can turn into an unmotivated asexual wife. You could also become an unmotivated asexual wife if you are an opinionated woman who does not listen to advice.

Women who have no interest in sex are often the most unspiritual and disobedient wives. Usually if your wife's main concern is to look angelic, good and impressive to the outside world, she will have no motivation to be a great sexual partner. Why do I say so? Because sexual activity is private and there are no people present there to praise you for your good show. There is no motivation to behave nicely.

Unmotivated Asexuals, often spend a lot of time to make themselves look good and impressive to the outside world. They desperately need to impress the world with their hair, their clothes and other pleasantries. Such people are oriented towards the external, the public and the outside.

The Beginnings

An Unmotivated Asexual will be very happy to get married and usually starts out by being apparently sexually excited. The desire to be pregnant is the motivation for sexual activity.

After having children, the asexual lady considers herself to be too busy for sexual excitement. At a point, she decides within herself that the sexual act is of no consequence.

After this decision, she makes no more effort to be sexually excited or involved. Over time, a complete disinterest in sex is established. She now avoids sex whenever possible and has sex as little as possible. When she does have sex, *The Unmotivated Asexual* does it with the least possible physical movement. An unmotivated asexual lady is unchanging and unresponsive to counselling.

Many Christian wives remain in their state of ignorance and rigidity when it comes to sexual matters. One day, I asked a devoted and spiritual Christian wife, "When was the last time you had sex with your husband?"

She answered, "Oh we have not had sex since our baby came."

"I see. How old is, your baby?" I asked.

She answered, "He is only eleven months old."

I continued, "So you have not had sex for the last eleven months?"

"No, we have not," she answered, looking at me quizzically. "Is there anything wrong?"

I paused and said, "I would not be surprised if your husband has another girlfriend whom he is sleeping with."

She was shocked at my answer and could not believe that I would say such a thing. But as time went on, I was proven right.

I thought to myself, this lady has had months and months of marriage counselling. She has been taught about the importance of sex and has had the benefit of reading Christian books on the subject. Somehow, she never really believed the teachings on why Christians must have active sexual lives. Many Christians simply do not understand that unbelievers live by different rules. If there is no sex at home, unbelievers just get it from somewhere else.

I remember another devoted Christian lady who was married to a pastor. Unfortunately for this pastor, he had married an unmotivated asexual lady. Unknown to her, her husband had also turned away and given himself to having sex with numerous other exotic and exciting ladies. He told me about how uninterested and unconcerned his wife was about sex.

He said, "She made no efforts at all and did not care if we hadn't had sex for weeks."

When his wife eventually found out about his lifestyle of fornication and adultery, she was understandably shocked, hurt, confused and appalled. But by the grace of God, their marriage was patched up and the pastor decided to live uprightly and stay away from his life of fornication.

One day, this husband travelled away for a ministry trip and was away for several weeks. Whilst he was away, he kept himself from every possible sexual sin and looked forward to going home to see his devoted Christian wife.

When he got home, his devoted wife was not in the mood for sex, even though he had been away for several weeks. He hungrily approached her, desiring to have her, since he had been away for so long. She told him that she was not ready for various reasons. She continued to give lame excuses for a whole week after her husband had arrived. She walked about in the home, completely uninterested, unprepared and unapproachable.

After some time she came across a senior pastor who casually asked about her sexual life. She smiled meekly and revealed that there had been no sex for several weeks. It was only upon the senior pastor's direct instructions that she went back home to have sex with her husband who had been starved of sex for almost three months.

This lady still did not understand the importance of sex in a Christian marriage. She did not understand how important it was for her to have sex often with her husband, the pastor.

The multiple affairs that her husband had had, had neither corrected nor improved the attitude of this unmotivated asexual lady. I will not be surprised if this pastor has more adulterous affairs in the future. Of course, he would be blamed, as usual, for his adultery. But this *Unmotivated Asexual* is a part of the problem. Remember that God sees all things. He does not just see one side. It is us human beings who see only one side of things.

The Beast

An established unmotivated and asexual woman has the following characteristics:

1. She does not like sex and does not want it. If she is married to an aggressive man, he will dictate the pace of sex. There will be numerous excuses why sex will not come on.

   I remember an *Unmotivated Asexual* who would call her children to the room when she sensed that her husband wanted to have sex with her. The presence of the children would act as a deterrent to the husband who would be unable to attempt having sex. These children became known as "the rescue team".

The Unmotivated Asexual says, "Does it have to come on?" She thinks of excuses that will work. One *Unmotivated Asexual* asked her husband for five hundred dollars before she would have sex with him.

Yet another unmotivated asexual lady kept her cheque book on the bedside table. When her husband, fully charged with his erection, was about to enter into his wife, she brought out the chequebook and asked him to sign a cheque first. The brother had to sign the cheque if he intended to continue. Indeed, some wives are even more expensive than prostitutes!

2. If *The Unmotivated Asexual* is married to a man who has had many exciting girlfriends in the past, she will completely deflate and demotivate him by her lack of interest.

3. *The Unmotivated Asexual* shows no feelings of warmth, does not touch her husband, cuddle up or kiss her husband.

    One day, an asexual and unmotivated lady was asked how her husband was able to have sex with her. "How does he have erections?" she was asked. "I do not know" she answered. "I do not know how he comes by his erections. He just comes with them."

4. An *Unmotivated Asexual* has almost no movement during sex. A slight wiggle or waggle is hardly noticeable in her pelvis. I remember one *Unmotivated Asexual* lady who fell asleep and began snoring while her husband was jumping on her having a self-generated experience of sex.

    Having sex with such a person is best compared with having sex with a cadaver. There are men who are known to have sex with cadavers, and marriage to *The Unmotivated Asexual* simulates closely the experience of people who have sex with dead bodies.

5. An *Unmotivated Asexual* does not make herself ready for sex. *The Unmotivated Asexual* gives off foul smells from the mouth, the vagina and the anus. She is unprepared and she

is unmotivated! Unclean, unkempt, and smelly vulvas and anuses are what her husband has to put up with. She is ready to bath when she wants to go out to impress the public; but there is no timely bathing or washing with *The Unmotivated Asexual* in preparation or expectation of sex. There is no timely brushing of teeth so that a kiss can be given. *The Unmotivated Asexual* presents herself just as she is. She may well be saying "Take me as I am!"

A pastor confided in his counsellor, "I can no longer have sex with my wife. The appearance of this woman just kills my desire." He continued, "My unmotivated and asexual wife presents herself to me with her stale urine, faeces, mucus, tissues and blood." She was unaware of her poor presentation and did not even know why her husband was no longer able to have sex with her.

6. The only sexual style deployed by *The Unmotivated Asexual* is to lie still on the bed, and join the mattress in its motionless state. One brother described his sex life like a bout of wrestling with an "unconscious patient". He had to manually lift his wife's arms, legs and torso into place, roll her over and arrange her in every necessary and suitable position.

Another brother described his struggles to move his wife around in the bed. "My wife's arms and legs arm are as heavy as five tubers of yam. I often wonder if I am a yam seller."

7. The main thoughts in *The Unmotivated Asexual* are, "When will it be over?" She is hopeful for a quick ejaculation from her spouse. *The Unmotivated Asexual* does not have orgasms! She has zero sexual feelings and does not want to have any either. The sensations that could have come from her body are absent. Orgasms are absent and happiness at the experience is also absent.

The Dangers

1. Deprivation: A pastor who is married to an unmotivated asexual lady is a highly deprived person. He will suffer from sexual starvation throughout his marriage. Some men suffer from food deprivation and hunger because their wives are not prepared to cook for them. Other men suffer from sexual deprivation.

   I have heard many stories about pastors and their marriages. I have spoken to two different pastors who wanted to be castrated.

   Once, a young pastor, full of desire told me how he was constantly refused sex by his cantankerous wife. Finally, he became frightened that he would end up committing adultery with an outsider. In his desperation, he had an idea. He said to himself, "If I am castrated, all my desires for sex will go away."

   So he decided to try and castrate himself. He went outside and took a blade and tried to cut his testicles off. Fortunately, it was too difficult and painful for him to cut off his testes. He was forced to abort his plan of self-castration.

   I warned his wife, "Do not think that you will escape with your wickedness towards your husband."

2. Memories: The pastor married to the asexual woman may have sweet memories of his past love relationships with exciting girlfriends. *The Unmotivated Asexual* is disinterested in sex and makes no effort to learn anything new or do anything exciting.

   Many times, sexual intercourse for the pastor reminds him of his past relationships. It leaves him with stronger relationship ties to former girlfriends with whom he has had many more happy times. One pastor remarked that he had had much more sex with his exciting past girlfriend than his unmotivated and asexual wife.

3. Pornography and masturbation: Unfortunately, due to the lack of excitement with his asexual wife, the pastor may turn to pornography and masturbation. Many are forced to fantasize with pornography as they "devour" the dead meat of their lady cadaver.

4. Fornication and adultery: In order to find excitement, the pastor discovers that there are others who are eager, energetic and willing to do any thing and every thing. He may become embroiled in affairs with other exciting young girls.

The unmotivated asexual Christian lady may realise that her husband is being driven away from her. One day, an unmotivated asexual lady told her husband (a pastor) as he was going out, "In case you have an affair with other girls just make sure you use condoms." Then she added, "And also make sure that any girl you sleep with does not become pregnant." This *Unmotivated Asexual* did not even care if her husband slept with any one. She just did not want to have the problem of stepchildren.

On another occasion, I spoke with a weeping pastor who had just committed adultery. The lady he had slept with was a church member and she had become pregnant. He sat by me weeping about his pathetic situation. With tears streaming down his face, he described what happens when he wanted to have sex with his unmotivated asexual wife.

He said, "She would take off her clothes, lie naked on the bed and say angrily, 'Okay, come!'"

He continued, "An angry naked woman is very different from a smiling naked woman. I had no appetite to jump on this angry naked woman."

Looking back, he realized that he had been driven away from his unwelcoming, unmotivated asexual woman, into the arms of a welcoming, motivated and sexy church usher.

Husbands who are married to unmotivated asexual girls, are in great danger of being subtly driven into the arms of outsiders. It may be happening to you but you may not realize what is going on. You must rise up and recognize that you are in a fight for your very life and ministry.

If you were an unbeliever banker, a computer analyst, a politician, a lawyer or a businessman, your morality may not matter much and it might also not affect your job. But when you are in the ministry, your morality affects your job greatly. When you fight to remain morally pure, you are fighting for your life and your ministry. Anything that threatens your morality threatens your ministry. Anything that threatens your morality threatens your job.

5. Disease: There are also health risks to the men who are forced to have less and less sex. Indeed, most men will have problems with their prostate glands at one point or the other. Statistics have it that, prostate cancer is reduced by sixty per cent in those who regularly have sex at least twenty-one times a month.

The *Unmotivated Asexual* inadvertently pushes her husband towards prostate disease. The unmotivated asexual lady's husband becomes more prone to diseases of the prostate and also more prone to an early death. She may cry at his funeral but probably contributed to his early death.

CHAPTER 21

What it Means to be Married to *A Quarrelsome Queen*

It is better to dwell in the wilderness, than with a contentious and an angry woman.

Proverbs 21:19

An odious woman is an outspoken lady who tends to quarrel with all and sundry. When she is married to a quiet man, she rules freely and determines the tone of her marriage through her quarrels.

Quarrelsome ladies may be a little extra beautiful. Perhaps, her beauty is a compensation for her poor character. If she were not so beautiful no one would ever marry her. The beauty of *Quarrelsome Queens* has fooled many a man.

Then the cover of lead was raised, and THERE IN THE BASKET SAT A WOMAN! He said, "THIS IS WICKEDNESS," and he pushed her back into the basket and pushed the lead cover down over its mouth

Zechariah 5:7-8 (NIV)

Many ministers are surprised to find that their beautiful, angelic wives have such bad character traits. Yes, she is stubborn and long discussions have to be held for her to change her mind on anything!

Before marriage, some brothers are actually impressed by the contentious attitude of the *"Quarrelsome Queen"*. They actually describe their bride as a woman of strong character who knows what she wants. What they do not realise is that the "strong character" is an ominous sign of her quarrelsome traits.

One of the first surprises will be the shock in finding how much the *Quarrelsome Queen* can shout. You will be shocked to find her shouting at everyone in the house.

This same person smiles gently and sweetly at everyone she meets in church. Many people think, "Pastor is really lucky to have this gentle angel as his wife." They have no idea that he is married to a *Quarrelsome Queen*.

Some *Quarrelsome Queens* do not shout at all but will contend against you by casting insinuations and having a negative attitude of silence and bitterness. It is as if they have mistakenly eaten a gall bladder. Non-shouting *Quarrelsome Queens* are equally wicked, prosecuting every little issue to its logical conclusion.

The *Quarrelsome Queen* has quarrels with different individuals, especially other ladies. When she meets up with fellow *Quarrelsome Queens*, there are fireworks and soon there is a long list of people who have had clashes with the pastor's wife.

Most of us do not associate wickedness with beautiful girls. You would have thought that an angelic beauty would be kind to house helps, maids and relatives. The pastor has to talk to her to show some kindness to his mother and sisters. She seems to want to have nothing to do with his family.

The Beast

1. The *Quarrelsome Queen* is an early starter. Since quarrelling is her nature, it comes out very early in their relationship or marriage. This wife develops a reputation for having quarrels with different people in the church.

   One day I visited a church which was pastored by a faithful older man who had married a younger beautiful lady.

   The pastor's wife was quite an outstanding beauty. I watched this pastor's wife smile sweetly and engage in little chitchats with everyone. She was quite conscious of her beauty and her appearance. When it was time for service, I noticed how she took an extra ten minutes to put on her make-up and fix her hair behind the stage. She couldn't seem to get enough paint on her face! Watch out for ladies who are extra conscious about how they look on stage, rather than how they behave at home.

   As events developed, I was amazed to find out that this beautiful pastor's wife who spent so much time dressing up behind the stage was actually a *Quarrelsome Queen*.

In fact, she had displayed such a bad attitude very early on in the marriage, during their honeymoon. During a discussion she was having with the bridegroom (her pastor) she jumped up in the wedding chamber and shouted at her husband and said, "I will not have any of this. I do not take nonsense from men!"

She continued, "I am experienced. I know men! I will not take nonsense from you or anyone!"

Then, she took off her wedding ring and threw it to the ground and stamped off in a fury. All this happened in the first few hours of their marriage. The pastor was dumbfounded and could not believe what was happening to him. He staggered into the adjoining chamber and made a phone call to a friend. He described what had just happened. His friend on the other end of the line was equally speechless. He whispered to the pastor, "I think you got the wrong one." Indeed, it turned out that he had gotten the wrong one.

I remember another beautiful lady who married a young missionary. She was an outstanding beauty and it was no surprise when she was selected by the young virgin pastor as his "beloved". After several months of counselling they got married and began their life together. With time it became difficult for her to hold back her quarrelling nature. During an argument, just four weeks into their marriage, she blurted out, "I shouldn't have married you!"

She continued, "I had other options! I shouldn't have married you!"

Then she said, "You are a small boy. You don't have anything!"

From then on, their wonderful marriage experienced the rude awakening of what it means to be a *Quarrelsome Queen*.

One of my missionaries married a beautiful *Quarrelsome Queen*. You should have seen them at their wedding! All bright and beautiful! Just three weeks into their marriage, the *Quarrelsome Queen* woke her husband up at dawn.

I know you are thinking that she woke her husband up to make love to him. After all they had been together for just twenty-one days.

Indeed, she woke him up at dawn because she was packing her bags to leave.

She told him, "I am leaving!"

She said to him, "You are somebody who has nothing!"

She continued, "I do not need you!"

Then she said, "You can report me to the pastors. I don't care. I will soon become immune to all your reporting."

This *Quarrelsome Queen* found her husband to be too slow and too indecisive. She pointed out to him, "You are not forceful enough and you never make the right decisions."

With that she was gone from the home and it took more than a year of counselling to get her to come back to her husband.

The Dangers

1. Failure: Pastors who are married to *Quarrelsome Queens* are often unsuccessful on the mission field because their wives are unable to blend in with the congregation and draw the members to her husband. Such wives do not attract the congregation to the church. They actually scatter the congregation in a very real way. The fruits of ministry must be borne in an atmosphere of peace.

   And the fruit of righteousness is sown in peace of them that make peace.

   James 3:18

One young pastor had the unfortunate experience of his young wife dying soon after they got married. He remarried another beautiful young lady and carried on with his mission.

After being married to his second wife for some time, I asked him, "How do you find this second marriage compared to the first?"

He said, "My second wife is better at sex than my first so I enjoy that part better."

He continued, "My first wife was very calm and quite non-sexual."

Then he continued, "My second wife is also quite quarrelsome. There is always one argument or another."

I paused. Then I asked him, "so, over all, which of the two wives do you prefer? The 'peaceful asexual wife' or the 'quarrelsome sexy wife'?"

He said, "I think I prefer the 'peaceful asexual' one!"

Amazing! This brother's testimony shows that peacefulness is a very important quality for a happy life. Do not underestimate the importance of peace in a marriage.

2. Confusion: A pastor who is married to a *Quarrelsome Queen* is unable to co-exist with other key families who are important to the mission. This is because his quarrelsome wife does not get along with the other families and often prevents the "family spirit" from developing.

3. Poverty: Indeed, a pastor who is married to a *Quarrelsome Queen* can expect poverty. He is likely to have limited success in ministry due to his wife's frequent quarrelling. She will scatter the very people who are important to his life.

He that is not with me is against me; and he that gathereth not with me scattereth abroad.

Matthew 12:30

4. Unanswered prayer: The pastor who is married to a *Quarrelsome Queen* can expect to have unanswered prayers. Misunderstandings and quarrels between the husband and wife can hinder prayers.

    Likewise, ye husbands, dwell with them according to knowledge, giving honour unto the wife, as unto the weaker vessel, and as being heirs together of the grace of life; THAT YOUR PRAYERS BE NOT HINDERED.

    1 Peter 3:7

5. Hatred: A pastor who is married to a *Quarrelsome Queen* can dislike his wife greatly for the contention she brings to his life. A pastor who is married to a quarrelsome lady can grow to dislike his wife for scattering important people from his life. He is in danger of being filled with hatred.

CHAPTER 22

What It Means to be Married to *A Relentless Accuser*

Wrath is cruel, and anger is outrageous; but who is able to stand before envy?

Proverbs 27:4

Marriage to a *"Relentless Accuser"* is the same as marriage to a *"Prison Officer"*.

A wife can become a *Prison Officer* with her chief weapon being her accusations! I call it a prison because the wife you have married can keep you in confinement. This confinement is caused by your *Prison Officer* wife who prevents you from interacting with people in the "outside world". To overcome in this kind of marriage, you need Joseph's anointing. It is Joseph who successfully came out of prison in Egypt.

You will be unable to relate to people that your wife does not like or does not want you to relate with. If your wife has the anointing of a *Prison Officer* she will use relentless accusations to keep you in confinement. The basic power that drives the *Prison Officer* is fear and jealousy or envy. Jealousy is a very powerful force. Jesus Christ was crucified because of envy. In the scripture above, jealousy is compared with anger and wrath. *Jealousy is more powerful, more cruel and more outrageous than anger and wrath!* A jealous and envious wife will use cruelty to eliminate nice people from your life.

John Wesley

John Wesley complained about being married to a prison officer. In his letter to his wife, he described the marriage to a 'prison officer' in great detail.

He wrote to his wife;

"I do not have a command of my own house.

I am not at liberty to invite even my nearest relative without angering you.

I dislike my chamber door being watched constantly, so that no one can go in and out except those you approve of.

I dislike being a prisoner even when I am away because I have to give an account of everywhere I go and of every person I ever speak to."

In the same letter, he asked for freedom from the prison. He wrote:

"Allow me liberty so that anyone who wants to, can come to me.

Let me go where I please and to whom I please without giving an account of it!

These are the advices I will now give you in the fear of God!"

"I DISLIKE BEING MYSELF A PRISONER IN MINE OWN HOUSE"

John Wesley

The first step towards imprisonment involves soft-spoken, subtle but negative comments about unwanted people.

The second step of the *Prison Officer* is to manipulate for the removal of people that she does not like or want. These people are forced to lose their positions of favour, their positions of closeness and even their jobs because of the manipulative powers of the 'Prison Officer' wife. The cruelty of envy is seen in the way people are mercilessly removed from their positions, no matter who they are. "Let them go to hell" is the unspoken cry of the *Prison Officer*. Once she does not see them in her life any more, she is at peace.

The third step for a *Prison Officer* manifests as violent accusations, violent quarrels and open confrontation about people who must go. One pastor said to me, "I've been accused of being interested in so many ladies, including my children's nanny. I have had to get rid of so many women who play important roles in my life."

He continued, "But I am also accused of being interested in men. I have had to get rid of several men in my life."

The Fearful Woman

There is no fear in love; but perfect love casts out fear, because fear involves punishment, and the one who fears is not perfected in love.

1 John 4:18 (NASB)

If you marry an insecure and fearful personality, you have entered the grounds of a *Relentless Accuser* Be careful of a woman who is only conscious of the presence of *"other nice ladies"*. Beware of a wife who is always thinking, "He could have married *her*. He wants *her*! He likes *her*! He prefers *her*! He is thinking about *her*! He wants to be with *her*! He likes talking to *her*! He is always on the phone to *her*! It's all about *her*!"

The accuser is preoccupied with *"other women"*. Instead of being preoccupied with *'other souls'* who need salvation, she is preoccupied with *'other women'* who "like" her husband! Usually, there is a reason why the "other woman" is of concern. She is often said to have a bad attitude towards the wife. She is usually accused of talking to the man of God but not to his wife. *The Prison Officer/Relentless Accuser* wants to get rid of this "other woman". She thinks to herself, "Go and get your own husband! Stop liking my husband!"

Then the cover of lead was raised, and there in the basket sat a woman! He said, "This is wickedness," and he pushed her back into the basket and pushed the lead cover down over its mouth.

Zechariah 5:7-8 (NIV)

I remember a Kenyan lady who married a man from Ghana. Instead of being happy and enjoying her husband's love, she continually accused him of wanting to marry someone from Ghana.

"You want a Ghanaian lady," she would say. "Is that not so? I know you want to eat your Ghanaian food."

"Go and get one of those Ghanaian girls", she would say.

You see, a *Prison Officer*, constantly makes references to girls from your country, your tribe or of your colour. She is not sure of your love! She senses the need to keep you for herself and she senses the need to keep you away from ladies she thinks are more suitable for you.

Why bother to take yourself through such emotional turmoil? Why marry someone you suspect does not really love you? Why live your life fearing that your husband loves other girls? Never marry someone whom you are suspicious of! You cannot be happily married unless there is absolute trust.

The *Prison Officer* and the Widower

It is not easy to be the new and second wife of a widower. Marrying a widower, means that you will have to step into the role of your husband's previous popular wife. Not everybody has the ability to become "the second wife". If you are insecure, you will always think about the first wife and what she did.

Your insecurity as a woman will manifest in you cleansing the world of supporters and lovers of the first wife. A new and insecure second wife is a sure candidate to becoming a *Prison Officer*.

Watch out for a woman who marries a pastor and feels that she is not accepted by the church. Such a person can turn into a *Prison Officer*.

I remember a pastor whose wife died suddenly. He married a young lady from the church and the trouble began. This new wife was so insecure that she fought against members of the church and even the children of the first wife. In the end, she drove the pastor's children away from him. The pastor's children were no longer welcome and could no longer work in the church.

Several key people in the administration of the church also had to leave. In the end, a very small fraction of the church was left. One of the pastors said to me, "We were blind. We had a *Relentless Accuser* in our midst and we did not deal with her. We now know that our pastor's wife was a *Prison Officer*. We should have fought and resisted her. We should have risen up when we could and put an end to the powers of this woman even though she was our senior pastor's wife."

He lamented, "By our lax attitude towards the *Prison Officer*, we lost all our members."

The *Prison Officer* and the Devoted Husband

Many women exhibit fear in one way or another and many become "Prison Officers". If you are a devoted "A1" husband (handsome, responsible, principled) you could be imprisoned by the *Prison Officer*!

The good qualities of devoted husbands are rare and the beautiful *Prison Officer* knows that she has a good thing. Unfortunately, a good and devoted "A1" husband may inspire *fear* and not *love* in his partner. Many people respond to love by being afraid.

I remember a pastor who attended an important four-day conference for ministers. He and his wife usually attended this conference with other pastors, friends and their wives. In the middle of the conference, the pastor abruptly decided to leave. Everyone was shocked that the pastor would leave before the conference ended. He gave no reasons and just departed, leaving his wife and other friends behind.

Two years later one of his friends asked him, "I remember how you mysteriously left that conference. What was the reason?"

He hesitated and then answered, "I couldn't take it any more, I was not enjoying the conference at all. Every time we came back to the hotel from the conference sessions, my wife was not happy with me."

"She was not happy because I was friendly towards your wife and other ladies. I don't think she likes it when I relate with any other ladies."

He continued, "It has always been an issue in our marriage."

"So what exactly made you leave?" he was asked.

"Well, one night whilst I was asleep, I opened my eyes and found my wife laying hands on me and casting out the spirit of adultery. I froze in the darkness of the hotel room and listened to the prayer that was being prayed over my head. I could not believe the prayers that were being said over my head."

The pastor continued, "My wife thought I was asleep so she took the liberty to administer deliverance to me whilst I was asleep."

This pastor continued lamenting and describing how he was constantly accused of unfaithfulness in spite of the fact that he had been faithful to his wife throughout their marriage.

He sighed, "That was the limit! After the laying on of hands and the midnight deliverance prayer I decided to leave the conference."

Such is the unfortunate lot of the man married to a *Prison Officer*. She cannot stand his interaction with any other female. She wants you for herself absolutely and totally. No gaps allowed! It is not easy to be in a prison, no matter how nice it looks! Even house arrest is a difficult thing. Every prisoner wants to be free. John Wesley had the same amazing experience in marriage. Please note these words he penned to his wife.

"I DISLIKE BEING BUT A PRISONER AT LARGE EVEN WHEN I GO ABROAD. INASMUCH AS YOU ARE HIGHLY DISGUSTED IF I DO NOT GIVE AN ACCOUNT OF EVERY PLACE I GO TO AND EVERY PERSON WITH WHOM I CONVERSE"

John Wesley

John Wesley's wife was completely focused on other women. She constantly accused him of having affairs with a string of other women. Mrs Wesley even accused John Wesley of having an affair with his brother, Charles Wesley's, wife.

Some "Prison Officers" become even more fearful at celebrations. Celebrations of the marriage and of love may provoke even more negative responses of fear from this type of person. The declaration of love to a *Prison Officer* frightens her even more and reminds her of how great a blessing she has, and how terrible it would be to lose it!

Why would a handsome man marry a beautiful lady full of fear, insecurity and jealousy? The answer is simple. It is very difficult to see a *Prison Officer* from the outside. Most of them do not wear uniforms. It is also difficult to imagine the torment you will have when you are married to a *Prison Officer*.

As a young unsuspecting man, you may notice her jealousy and feel that you are really loved. Only a discerning person can see through the disguise of a future *Prison Officer*.

I remember a beautiful young wife who made a comment to her husband after he finished preaching. She simply remarked, "I am sure Felicia enjoyed your sermon." Instead of saying she was blessed by his sermon, her mind was on Felicia who was also in church that day!

It is amazing that a beautiful lady can harbour vices like insecurity, jealousy and hatred. All these vices exist within the beauty but are completely submerged beneath the charm. Only the trained eye will notice the signs of looming trouble.

A gentle, soft-spoken personality is the perfect camouflage for the *Prison Officer*.

Stay in Prison

The main effect of this kind of marriage is to keep you under control by accusing you about every possible lady. If you employ someone, your wife will be against the person; male or female. If you like someone, your wife will dislike that person. If you have a good relationship with someone, your wife will not have a good relationship with that person.

I remember a pastor's wife who fought all the employees and relationships that her husband had developed in order to keep him to herself. Perhaps she just existed to accuse! This beautiful pastor's wife attempted to change the records on the telephone bills to fabricate evidence that her husband was having affairs with some church members. She was desperate to prove that her husband was calling young girls at midnight. Fortunately, she was unable to get the telephone company to change the telephone records for her to justify her false accusation.

The Control of an Accuser

For as many as are led by the Spirit of God, they are the sons of God.

Romans 8:14

You must be led by the Holy Spirit and not by a woman. The most dangerous thing about a *Prison Officer* is her ability to control your life. The most deadly danger of a *Prison Officer* is her ability to "take over" from the Holy Spirit. The *Prison Officer* takes over from the Holy Spirit and leads you into the path she has chosen. Many curses were released into the world when Adam turned from following God to following his wife.

And unto Adam he said, Because thou hast HEARKENED UNTO THE VOICE OF THY WIFE, and hast eaten of the tree, of which I commanded thee, saying, Thou shalt not eat of it: CURSED is the ground for thy sake; in sorrow shalt thou eat of it all the days of thy life;

Genesis 3:17

The mind of your beautiful *Prison Officer* wife works like a character in a soap opera, constantly discussing and analysing different affairs and scandals. The dangerous thought patterns of the soft-spoken beauty are seen in her comments and innuendos. She has a strong awareness of the ever-present love affairs, scandals, adulteries and betrayals that exist in the world.

Indeed, the *Prison Officer* fights for control and dominance with every possible tool. She threatens her husband with the consequence of having sex with other ladies. I remember one lady who said to her husband, "If you dare fornicate with someone you will lose your anointing."

Some "Prison Officers" use hysteria to threaten the poor pastor. A certain wife was known to throw herself on the floor, screaming and rolling all over the living room floor. Outsiders would run into the house to find out what was happening, only to find the man of God's wife on the floor, screaming and rolling.

Indeed, what an embarrassment and indictment on the pastor. What did he do to make his wife scream and roll? What was happening? What evil was going on between the pastor and his wife? Outsiders would naturally think, "This must be a bad pastor to have caused such a gentle beauty to scream and roll all over the house!" Obviously, the pastor would back down and try to do everything to prevent the screaming and the rolling.

The *Prison Officer* also has a political mind that instantly sees things in groups and parties: my friends-your friends, my relatives-your relatives, my staff-your staff, my people-your people, my mother-your mother, my father-your father!

A Prison Officer's political mind is constantly searching and suspiciously diagnosing the likes and dislikes of people. It is revealed when she describes her opinion of your likes and dislikes. She is always suspiciously looking out for whom she thinks you like.

For instance, she will say things like; "You like chicken". "You like rice." "You like fair people." "You like boys from Spartan College." "You like girls from Victoria Girls' High School".

Such a person will notice the different tribes or groupings within a group. For instance, such a person may say, "Everybody in the new government is from the Western Region." "Everybody in the new government is Yoruba."

In the same way, the *Prison Officer* will quickly identify the people that she thinks her husband likes. Then, with her sick mind, she will proceed to accuse, intimidate and harass the poor man about these people. "You like Freda. You like Samantha. You like Jessica. You like Vanessa. You like Esmeralda. You like Winifred" !!!!!!!

Usually, there are some names of people that the poor husband is accused of being interested in. The presence of these prominent names makes the accusations seem valid. In the case of John Wesley, his wife constantly accused him about two or three particular ladies. Names like Betty Disine, Sarah Crosby and Sarah Ryan are mentioned as women that John Wesley is supposed to have been interested in.

What You Can Expect

The *Prison Officer* will frown upon the kindness and attention you show to any other lady in your life. Initially, it may be a mild frown. As time progresses and as respect diminishes, the frown will develop into open disapproval characterised by pointed questions.

If the soft-spoken aspersions are successful in curtailing relationships, they will continue. As and when a new girl shows up, these accusations will be revived. Most of the time, the manipulative power of accusations is strong enough to control a principled young man who loves the Lord and wants to have a good marriage.

There are, however, some ladies who are not prepared to stop at subtle comments, suggestions or even direct accusations. Such women break out into openly aggressive and violent accusations. If you have married such a woman she will openly confront people she does not like.

I remember one lady who went to the home of her husband's assistant with a team of supporters to confront the lady whom she suspected of being in love with her husband. They arrived with a warlike team to warn the lady to stay off her husband.

One pastor said to me, "My wife has had so many confrontations with so many women in the church. I have to bow my head in shame because of my wife."

Such a lady will openly confront church members, relatives or even bystanders whom she suspects of having even the faintest interest in her husband.

I remember one wife who would confront parents from her children's school on the school's car park. The bewildered parent would stumble away not knowing what the confrontation was about.

From the very beginning the *Prison Officer* will find something wrong with many external friendships. She will find something wrong with the choir leader, the worship leader and all other people that you worked happily with before she came on the scene. As time goes on, more and more people will be added to the list of unacceptable relationships.

You can expect to have many quarrels with your wife over the different people you work with. If one were listening outside the window of this couple's bedroom, one would think that you had stumbled into arguments about a real affair. In reality however, it may be just an argument about a *Prison Officer's* suspicions, imaginations and delusions.

Kathryn Khulman and the *Prison Officer*

In the life story of Kathryn Khulman, we see how she travelled with her sister who was married to an evangelist. She had a first hand glimpse into her sister's marriage. A stormy marriage is what we read about but the details are even more revealing. Kathryn Khulman's sister, Myrtle, was constantly accusing her husband of consorting with other women. She became more and more hard and unyielding with time. Kathryn Khulman said her sister reminded her of their mother who had been equally hard and unyielding to her father.

I have met several pastors who have had to relieve different ladies from positions of importance to appease their wives. In his quest to walk in love towards his wife, the pastor will agree to get rid of "suspected lovers". The first one will go and the second will follow soon. One after another, the different ladies will be removed from every place of importance. Soon, you will have a long list of ladies who have been removed from every position of importance.

One such lady was rebuked by her daughter. She said to her mother, "Is the list of women that you claim Daddy to be in love with, not too long?"

Amazingly, this pastor was accused by his wife of being in love with ladies who even belonged to other religions.

Another daughter said of her mother, "My mother has accused my father of being in love with so many women including our aunties and other relatives. Even people who could be aunties to Daddy have been included in the list."

One pastor remarked to me, "I have been accused of having something to do with both ladies and men."

It is not a small thing to spend your life with someone who believes that you are having an affair. You will never have a certain kind of happiness from your relationship and marriage!

One day I was standing with a great man of God whose wife had been accusing him of having affairs with a long list of ladies. He said to me, "Can you believe that my wife called me tonight to warn me about an eighty-two year old lady who was attending this programme?"

My jaw dropped in disbelief because I knew the lady he was talking about. This woman was a jolly round great grandmother.

He continued, "She said to me over the phone, 'Don't forget I have warned you many times about that woman. I know she is after you. She wants to have sex with you. She will not stop chasing you till she gets you.'"

Even though she was miles away, this *Prison Officer* was controlling her husband through warnings, accusations and suggestions. The *Prison Officer* earnestly seeks to keep you in confinement, even though she is far away.

The Dangers of Being Married to a *Prison Officer*

1. Accusations: You are in danger of becoming an accuser yourself. You may respond to the accusations with an equally matched accusation. Many people feel that they are justified in getting divorced or separated from a *Prison Officer*. They say, "No one would be able to endure what I am enduring in this marriage." Be very careful that you do not respond in the wrong way. Notice this amazing scripture:

Answer not a fool according to his folly, lest thou also be like unto him.

Proverbs 26:4

2. Strife: You must watch out for the dangers of strife. The Bible warns that the fruit of righteousness must be sown in the midst of peace by those who make peace.

And the fruit of righteousness is sown in peace of them that make peace.

James 3:18

3. Bitterness: You must also watch out for the dangers of bitterness and hatred. It is natural to dislike someone who accuses you constantly. It is not natural to love someone who accuses you. Only the supernatural love of God can make you love your accuser and that is what you must pray for.

4. Lust: You must watch out for the dangers of lust. Everyone notices things that are pointed out to you. When your wife accuses you about a lady, you will notice her more than the other ladies. One day you may say, "Since that is what they are expecting of me, I might as well do it." You may become a fornicator although you never intended to.

5. Divorce: You must watch out for the dangers of divorce. As your home turns into a place of bitter contention, you will desire to be away from it. You may find solace and peace in the company of trusting and loving people. Through this forced disassociation with your wife, you may develop other relationships. You may have an affair you do not intend to have. You may separate from your wife and you may end up divorced. Remember that this is satan's ultimate plan and you must ensure that it does not happen.

I declare you to be an overcomer in every prison you find yourself in. Receive the anointing of Joseph who overcame in the prison!

CHAPTER 23

What it Means to be Married to *The Unyielding Opposer*

Be sober, be vigilant; because YOUR ADVERSARY the devil, as a roaring lion, walketh about, seeking whom he may devour:

1 Peter 5:8

S atan is called your adversary. *"Adversary"* simply means someone who opposes you. The one who opposes you and stops you in your tracks is your adversary. Unfortunately, some wives take up satan's job and become the main opposition to the man of God.

In this kind of marriage, satan goes on holiday as the pastor's wife takes over the job of opposing her husband in everything he does. There is now no need of the devil in the marriage because his work is being handled by an *"Unyielding Opposer"*.

I remember a young married doctor who travelled to Europe to specialise in medicine. Shortly after he began his specialisation, he heard the call of God and felt that he should give himself to ministry rather than to being a doctor. Unfortunately, he had married an *Unyielding Opposer*. Even though he was blessed with a large church in Europe, the *Unyielding Opposer* gave her husband hell.

She chided him, she fought him and she opposed him constantly about his decision to be in the ministry. This man suffered terribly because his wife would not support him. He experienced hell at home because his wife was intent on stopping him from being in the ministry. She wanted to be married to an ordinary doctor and live a "normal" life. Eventually, the marriage broke down and they went their separate ways.

Complaining and Discontentment

The type of lady that becomes an *Unyielding Opposer* is usually a complaining, discontented person with little understanding about complex issues. Because of her shallowness and sometimes lack of education, she fails to understand the need to submit. Her beauty was a perfect lure for the unsuspecting man of God.

You may be a young man who meets this beautiful lady and is impressed with her charm and beauty. After a short courtship, you commit yourself because you are impressed by her seemingly good qualities. During your courtship, both she and her family are fully compliant. She welcomes you into her life and seems to be the most trusting, compliant and obedient person you have ever met. But it does not take long for the discontentment and complaints to surface.

> **Then the cover of lead was raised, and there in the basket sat a woman! He said, "This is wickedness," and he pushed her back into the basket and pushed the lead cover down over its mouth.**
>
> **Zechariah 5:7-8 (NIV)**

When John Wesley got married, his wife decided to travel with him. She soon made everyone aware of the difficult conditions under which John Wesley travelled. The pouring rain, the driving winds, the cold winter, the stones thrown by angry mobs and the taunts of jeering antagonists! On one occasion, when she arrived at the site of the meeting, she and John were met by a group of adoring women, all arrayed in their beautiful clothes.

Two things bothered John Wesley's wife immediately:

1. She was concerned that she did not look so nice after a fifty-mile ride on horseback,

2. She was concerned that the women gathered around her husband showed no interest in her but in her husband.

After the church service, John Wesley was full of the Spirit, praising God for all the spiritual blessings of the trip. But she complained about the hard beds, the itchy bed covers that were too small and the insects that were in the room. There are people who complain about everything! Because of this complaining attitude, John Wesley stopped travelling with her.

Another thing that John Wesley's wife complained about was that she was not liked by the Methodist ministers. The Methodist leadership had noticed that their founder had a bad deal in his marriage. Obviously, the Methodists loved their leader so they began to resent this woman.

Mrs Wesley wrote to her husband and said, "For God's sake, for your sake, put a stop to this torrent of evil (from the Methodist ministers) that is poured out against me."

There are certain groups of people who are more prone to quarrels. These unyielding personalities may come from tribes that are well known for contentious and senseless, unending family quarrels. In such families, uncles fight against uncles and aunties quarrel with each other until they enter their graves.

Some countries are known to have aggressive women who are strong, manly and even violent. Gentleness and softness are not natural to them. You would never imagine that the beauty sitting in front of you could turn into a *Wild Cat* at the least provocation.

During the relationship, most quarrels are quickly resolved and both parties move on, hopeful that in marriage there will be no lasting point of disagreement. However, after marriage, one thing after another leads to the manifestations of discontentment, complaints, stubbornness and unyieldingness.

The Stubborn Beast

As time goes by, the beauty you have married will appear to dislike whatever you like. Her husband will often say, "If my wife agrees then it must be from God", because she never agrees to anything. Your wife becomes your number one opposer! Opposition parties never agree to what the ruling government says.

John Wesley pleaded with his wife to change! John Wesley lectured his wife. When his pleadings and lectures did not work, he just ignored her.

John Wesley could persuade most women but he was unable to convince his wife, Molly. John Wesley once made a comment about his wife,

"ONE MIGHT AS WELL TRY TO CONVINCE THE NORTH WIND…"

John Wesley

The stubborn *Unyielding Opposer* has an answer for everything and never understands anything! Unlike the church members, who seem to understand everything the pastor says, she never seems to agree with his viewpoint. It's amazing to see wives who have become icons of opposition. The beautiful flow they once had when he was leading her around like a lamb is gone.

She says to him, "I am not one of those girls in the church."

She will refer to the church members as "Your fans" and "Your people". She never says "Yes" to an issue to which she should say "Yes". She never says "No" when the answer should be "No"! She never agrees! She never bows! She never gives in! The home of such a couple is the centre of arguments and unresolved issues.

Many years ago, I attended an ordination service in a friend's church. The minister preached powerfully about the need to sacrifice for the ministry. At a point, he became teary and began to cry. He explained that the ministry had cost him so much. He described how he came back home one day from a trip and his wife sat him down for a short meeting.

She said to him, "I want a normal husband!"

She continued, "I don't want a husband who travels all the time, away on preaching missions."

"But I have to fulfil my ministry," he explained.

"Well, I want a normal husband and if you will not be a normal husband, I can't continue to be your wife."

Try as he could, he was never able to convince her to stay. That was the end of their marriage. This *Unyielding Opposer* forced this man into a divorce.

I watched in amazement as the pastor wept in front of the whole congregation. He had been abandoned by his wife and was broken by the experience. His wife would simply not follow him nor support him. As he ordained these new pastors, he warned them that they should be ready for surprises in the ministry.

Then the cover of lead was raised, and *there in the basket sat a woman!* He said, *"This is wickedness,"* and he pushed her back into the basket and pushed the lead cover down over its mouth.

Zechariah 5:7-8 (NIV)

The Dangers

For where envying and strife is, there is confusion and every evil work.

James 3:16

1. Strife: Unyielding opposers generate lots of strife. Wherever there is strife, there are many other evil works. Peace is very important and "the fruit of righteousness must be sown in peace by those who make peace".

2. Bitterness and unforgiveness are common evils in such marriages. Attempts by the wife to usurp a husband's authority and take over his leadership role are common. Marriage to an unyielding opposer is like leading a nation of enemies.

3. Separation: Husband and wives may try to create separate worlds so that they can co-exist peacefully.

Sometimes, another world must be created so that this beast will be able to live and function apart from her husband, without having her constantly challenging and opposing him.

Sometimes, such couples live in different countries or in different cities so that they can continue to refer to each other as man and wife. Some couples even attend different churches so that they can go back home to relate to each other peacefully.

CHAPTER 24

What it Means to be Married to *a Loveless Oldie*

Go and cry in the ears of Jerusalem, saying, Thus saith the Lord; I remember thee, the kindness of thy youth, the love of thine espousals, when thou wentest after me in the wilderness, in a land that was not sown.

Israel was holiness unto the Lord, and the firstfruits of his increase: all that devour him shall offend; evil shall come upon them, saith the Lord.

Jeremiah 2:2-3

I once sat by a fifty-eight year old pastor who was reminiscing about his broken marriage. He described how his wife would take the stage and speak so sweetly to the congregation. He said, "My wife was charming and very beautiful. The congregation just loved her. She was like an angel."

He continued, "She would say to the church, 'I just love my wonderful husband and children. They are so precious to me.'"

Then he said, "Every time she said things like that from the stage, I wanted to jump up and scream, 'You are a liar! You are a liar! You are a liar!'"

He continued, "She did not love me. You should see how she treated me at home. An angel at church and a beast at home!"

He ended by saying, "To have a bit of sex, I had to negotiate and virtually beg."

It is interesting to observe the passionate love between young couples and the passivity that exists between *Loveless Oldies*. Lovers seem to go on a long journey from "first love" to *Loveless Oldies*.

Love and marriage can go through amazing deterioration. Jeremiah 2:2 is the classic scripture that describes the deterioration of love. In the scripture above, the Lord laments to Jerusalem about the changes that have taken place in their relationship.

He says, *"I remember the kindness of your youth."* Many ladies are very kind in their youth. Many older experienced wives are not so kind to their husbands. They often seem irritated with their troublesome husbands. Is it any wonder that the older men go around looking for young girls?

The Lord goes on to remember *"the love of thine espousals."* This means the love of 'thy bridehood'. Many older men long for the love of a young and exciting bride. All they are left with is a dried up, old and bitter woman.

The last problem that the Lord lamented about was how she no longer sought him, followed him and desired him. He said, *"I remember when thou wentest after me in the wilderness."* How nice it is for the girl to go after the man she loves. Many pastors desire their wives to initiate love as it was in the days of the first love.

Many men long to be desired and loved. Instead, they are tolerated and accommodated.

Unfortunately, the man who was once desired is now seen as a bother and a source of irritation. This same lady was once out there seeking for a husband. She was looking for love. She would attend prayer meetings and seek the pastor's help. "Please help me to find a husband. Please choose someone for me. Please do you know anyone who could marry me? Please recommend me to someone. Pastor, will I get married this year? Please bless me! I really want a husband. Anyone will do!"

This was the cry of the woman seeking love. Today, she is irritated when her husband tries to touch her. She cannot stand the constant inconvenience that he brings to her life. She considers him to be a nuisance. Amazing!

Our love for God easily deteriorates. That is why God knows all about deteriorating love. He experiences it from us all the time. When love deteriorates, you are just left with a *Loveless Oldie*. The Lord is our lover. Everything to do with God has to do with love. He loves us and He expects us to love him passionately. All through the Bible, God refers to His people as people He has married.

Turn, O backsliding children, saith the Lord; FOR I AM MARRIED UNTO YOU:...

Jeremiah 3:14

For THY MAKER IS THINE HUSBAND; the Lord of hosts is his name; and thy Redeemer the Holy One of Israel; The God of the whole earth shall he be called.

Isaiah 54:5

This wonderful relationship we have with the Lord deteriorates just like human marriage relationships deteriorate. A deteriorating marriage goes through these amazing stages until you end up with a *Loveless Oldie*. It is important to study the stages of deterioration of nice marriages. Each of these stages is distinct and worth understanding. *(See chapter 14)*

It is time to remember the virtues of Ruth. Boaz recommended Ruth for showing even more kindness in the latter stages of her life. Most people show less love in the latter stages of their lives. Less love, less romance, less kindness, less tolerance, less obedience, less humility in the latter stages of their lives! God is telling you that you can show kindness when you are older. Boaz decided to marry Ruth because she was a lady who could show love and kindness when she was older. Many young, cheerful, giggly and eager girls can show intense love. But how many of these eager young girls will show love when they are older?

And when Boaz had eaten and drunk, and his heart was merry, he went to lie down at the end of the heap of corn: and she came softly, and uncovered his feet, and laid her down.

And it came to pass at midnight, that the man was afraid, and turned himself: and, behold, a woman lay at his feet. And he said, Who art thou? And she answered, I am Ruth thine handmaid: spread therefore thy skirt over thine handmaid; for thou art a near kinsman.

And he said, Blessed be thou of the Lord, my daughter: for THOU HAST SHEWED MORE KINDNESS IN THE LATTER END THAN AT THE BEGINNING, inasmuch as thou followedst not young men, whether poor or rich.

And now, my daughter, fear not; I will do to thee all that thou requirest: for all the city of my people doth know that thou art a virtuous woman.

Ruth 3:7-11

CHAPTER 25

What it Means to be Married to *The Uncaring Independent*

There is difference also between a wife and a virgin. The unmarried woman careth for the things of the Lord, that she may be holy both in body and in spirit: but she that is married careth for the things of the world, how she may please her husband.

1 Corinthians 7:34

Independent Women

A well-educated woman once said to me, "I am fiercely independent!" A choleric and outspoken personality can easily metamorphose into an uncaring and independent beauty.

Once our humble beauty becomes financially independent, she could easily metamorphose into an *Uncaring Independent* woman.

The Beauty

A young man is blown off his feet by this beautiful lady who has all the qualities that he is looking for. Her well-formed figure plays on his testosterone-influenced mind and he says to himself, "I have found what I need". In this newfound love, he sees strength of character and is attracted to it. He is drawn to this decisive woman who exudes so much confidence. Because she is decisive and strong, she seems to know everything and to have the solutions to all of life's problems. He moves forward and seizes the moment by getting married to this beautiful lady.

John Wesley described how his wife gave him the most *intense and inviolable affection* before they got married. However, she was completely independent and walked out on him a number of times in a bad temper, vowing, "You will see me no more!"

"YOU WILL SEE ME NO MORE!"

Mrs. Molly Wesley

The Uncaring Independent is difficult to reach and often busier than the man. She is a career woman with a vision. She knows what she wants to accomplish with her life. Being a career woman, she has no time for useless socializing. She also does not have much time for soft love talks.

If you are in love with an *Uncaring Independent*, expect her to "agree" that she is in love but do not expect her to demonstrate it much. She may receive many lessons on how to love but all to no avail. You will send a lot of texts and messages to her but she will send very few back to you.

The Beast

The Uncaring Independent is a busy woman, she has things to achieve, and she loves her work more than she loves her husband! She finds fulfilment at work but considers all her domestic chores mundane and boring.

When her husband is sick, she tells him where he can find medicine and where to find some food. Her husband, the man of God becomes like a woman, taking the children to school, looking after them, whilst the *Uncaring Independent* beauty goes about achieving her goals.

The Uncaring Independent is always on the phone to somebody, always sending emails and texts. She is always organizing something in the world. Her husband feels like a fly in the midst of the busy world of this "uncaring independent beauty".

After marriage, she realises that the pastoral and tender heart of her husband is ready to accept many inconveniences. She recognizes that she can capitalize on the softness and kindness of her husband.

Soon, she is in absolute control and runs the home and their lives and takes decisions on behalf of the household. She becomes the director in charge of affairs.

As time goes on, the *Uncaring Independent* may become rude and flippant in her communication to her husband. She can correct him at any time, argue with him and walk off.

Remember, that he has become an unimportant fly, with whom she has had to associate for social reasons. Her sharp tongue is used to correct, belittle and humiliate her patient, loving and desire-filled husband.

The Post-Donation Syndrome

The pastor wants to relax with his beautiful wife. He wants to rest his head on her lap, but she does not like being touched. The poor husband of the *Uncaring Independent* desires her all the time but she has no need of him sexually.

After all, he has donated his sperms and helped her to have the children she wanted. The sex act, when it is not being done for the sake of having a child is seen as a meaningless and inconvenient intrusion.

To the *Uncaring Independent*, sexual intercourse may be likened to sticking a wooden stick up the anus of an individual who is politely minding his own business. And who would like the inconvenience of having a stick shoved up his anus? No one enjoys such inconveniences! The *Uncaring Independent* certainly does not want such inconveniences!

This couple will enjoy sex based on the decisions and timing that suit Madam Boss. The gentle requests by her meek husband are shoved aside. As and when she thinks it is appropriate to have sex with her husband, the "show" comes on.

If her husband has been sent to a mission field, she will put her foot down and say, "I am not going." She has gotten used to having her own way. Instead of being a humble spouse that follows, submits and yields to her husband's vision, she has become an unyielding, uninterested and independent partner.

I know of a number of wives of missionaries who simply told their husbands that they would not come to the mission field. Some even left their husband's side and travelled away independently on their own private agenda. What a shock!

In some cases, the wives would travel to the western world and eventually the poor husband, in need of money and sex, would be forced to leave the mission field to join her wherever she was.

The Dangers

1. Lack of comfort: To be married to an *Uncaring Independent* is to enter into a "fend-for-yourself" marriage. You have to care, love and comfort yourself, as you will not receive these from your uncaring independent wife. She has no time for soft words. She has no time for frivolous time wasting. She has no time for leaning on you, lying on you or cuddling up to you. She is moulded in a *cast iron soul*, with little or no feelings. Her breasts are simply for breast-feeding and nothing else!

The Spirit of a Giraffe

To survive in such a marriage, you need the "spirit of a giraffe". A giraffe lives without comfort and sleeps on its feet. A giraffe never lies down because it is too dangerous. God will give you the grace of a giraffe so that you can live without resting. Through this grace, you will be able to live your life without comfort, without care and without love.

2. Resentment: The pastor will grow to resent his wife for despising him. The man of God can become hostile towards his wife, as he tries to rise up and challenge his lofty wife.

3. Fighting: When a man is unable to stand up to the sharp words that come from the "headmistress" that he has married, he may resolve to hitting her.

    Unable to speak as quickly as she does, he may use his hands to strike her. Unable to come up with as many provocative words as she does, a slap or two may be his response!   In the end, the man of God will be accused of physical violence while misguidedly trying to beat his gentle wife into submission.

4. Desertion: Many quiet husbands tolerate a lot of mistreatment from their domineering, uncaring, self-asserting and independent wives. But there are some husbands who,

after a long period of non-response, suddenly react with an irreversible and absolute departure from the marital home.

I know several meek husbands who left their wives suddenly after enduring emotional and psychological domination for years. They silently walked away, got themselves a new dwelling place and lived there, away from the presence of their domineering headmistress.

Often, this came as a shock to the *Uncaring Independent* who thought that her sheep-like husband would always stay under her powers. Somehow, she didn't think that far!

CHAPTER 26

What it Means to be Married to *A Divorce-Prone Beauty*

My son, fear thou the Lord and the king: and meddle not with them that are given to change.

Proverbs 24:21

There are some women who do not have the ability to marry. Their personalities are incompatible with a marriage setting. Anyone who gets into a marriage with such a person is sure to be divorced after a while. These are women who are creators of divorce and I call them *"Divorce-Prone Beauties"*.

If you ever marry one of these, you have married someone whose very life and behaviour will cause a divorce to happen. The *Divorce-Prone Beauty* is a woman who is sent into your life to marry you so that you will be forced into divorce one day. Through your marriage to her, you are certain to become a divorcee.

One day, as I looked upon a certain lady, the Holy Spirit whispered to me, "Anyone who marries this lady will get divorced." Some people have an "unmarriageable evil spirit" in them. It takes a certain spirit of humility, love, obedience and holiness to enter into marriage and stay married. Some people do not have what it takes to be married. It is simply a defect in their souls.

Also, there are countries and cultures that are more prone to divorce than others. In some countries, the women are very strong and very independent. Sometimes the women are like strong aggressive men. If you look closely, you will find that the women in these places rarely get married. They may have sex and they may have children but they do not get married.

A doctor friend of mine told me about a clinic that he runs in a particular community in the United States. He said, "It is rare for a couple (husband and wife) to come to the clinic with their child."

He said to me, "All the children I see in the clinic belong to single mothers. There are no fathers to most of these children."

A teacher once told us about a school that he worked for on some islands. On this island, it was only foreigners whose children had two parents! Every single local child in the school was from a home with a single mother. After four years of working there, he still did not have any students who had both a father and mother staying together.

There are many reasons for such situations. Sometimes, it is irresponsible men who just impregnate women and run off. At other times, the women are *Divorce-Prone Beauties* who simply do not know how to live with a man. It is possible that many of the women on this island simply could not submit themselves to a man and be humble wives.

Woe to you if you marry any of these *Divorce-Prone Beauties*! Your possible days of a happy marriage are limited. You will soon receive your marching orders from a difficult, unyielding, unsubmissive, uncompromising, inflexible, stubborn, defiant, belligerent, bad-tempered, argumentative, challenging, confrontational, quarrelsome, distrustful, suspicious, aggressive, irritable and hostile woman.

A man of God described how happy his marriage was until he found himself in a divorce court. He pleaded with his wife to stay with him, but she would not. This man of God was forced to divorce his wife after ten years of marriage even though he did not want to. He had married a *Divorce-Prone Beauty* but he did not know it. Whilst in court, his wife smiled at him and sent him texts him from the other side of the bench saying, "I love you."

Another great man of God described to me how he begged his wife not to leave him. "Please don't leave," he said. But she would have none of it.

He told me that his children came to join in the pleas. "Please don't leave Daddy" they said. One of the children told their mother, "You have taught us for many years that we should obey the Word of God. Please obey the Word of God now and don't divorce our daddy."

But she would have none of that and insisted on divorcing.

Once upon a time I was in Asia and I had the privilege of having dinner with a great man of God. He described a divorce situation that he had encountered close up. He described how his pastor's wife had had an affair with her boyfriend. His pastor was so provoked by his wife's affair and ended up also having an affair with someone else.

He said to me, "On hindsight, the best thing my pastor should have done was to have divorced his wife. But he could not bring himself to divorce his wife even though she was sleeping with friends right under his nose."

He continued, "My pastor was so concerned about his reputation that he refused to divorce his wife even though he had the biblical grounds of adultery. Instead, of divorcing his wife, he got himself a girlfriend to avenge his wife's behaviour. Unfortunately, this only brought him more trouble."

Many men of God enter into marriage with ladies who are incompatible with ministry and marriage. Just as people have defects in their kidneys, hearts or livers, some women have defects in their souls and are unable to marry. There are some women who do not have the ability to marry!

Surprisingly, many pastors prefer to carry on living with their adulterous wives than to get a divorce. Only a few husbands are bold enough to leave. I can understand that because no one will really believe that you have any good reason for getting divorced. People will secretly think that you are having an affair with someone else! Amazingly, God Himself decided to divorce Israel when He could not take it any more. Notice the scriptures below, which show how God took the decision to divorce Israel.

> Thus saith the Lord, Where is the bill of YOUR MOTHER'S DIVORCEMENT, whom I have put away? or which of my creditors is it to whom I have sold you? Behold, for your iniquities have ye sold yourselves, and for your transgressions is your mother put away.
>
> Isaiah 50:1

And I saw, when for all the causes whereby backsliding Israel committed adultery I HAD PUT HER AWAY, AND GIVEN HER A BILL OF DIVORCE; yet her treacherous sister Judah feared not, but went and played the harlot also.

Jeremiah 3:8

When faced with such a difficult situation, it may be better for you to be like John Wesley and remain separated and unmarried till you die. You must realise that people have an inherent mistrust for men when it comes to marriage and relationships. Even when a pastor's wife is dead, people are not happy when he remarries. They think that he is not showing love and respect to his wife by marrying again.

The Dangers

1. Divorce and Loss of Favour: The dangers to the man of God are many. People rarely understand and accept a divorced person. He finds himself in a kind of trap, between a rock and a hard place. When he tries to explain himself, no one believes him. Upon divorcing his wife he loses favour with many important people and even with the congregation. This is the great danger of marrying a *Divorce-Prone Beauty*. You enter into a divorce you never bargained for.

2. A Stormy Marriage: The pastor married to a *Divorce-Prone Beauty* may have a stormy marriage. The children in such marriages are greatly affected by living in a tumultuous situation.

3. Revenge: Some pastors are so provoked by their wife's behaviour that they decide to revenge by having affairs with other ladies. This type of sexual retaliation only leads to more complications. As the Bible says, "Do not respond to a fool according to his folly otherwise you will become the same as him." By responding to the provocation of your spouse, you become just like her.

CHAPTER 27

What it Means to be Married to *The Patient*

Beloved, I wish above all things that thou mayest prosper and be in health, even as THY SOUL PROSPERETH.

3 John 2

The Beauty

When your soul prospers, your mind, your emotions and your feelings are well. Many pastors marry apparently normal beautiful ladies. Unfortunately, some ladies do have a mental illness. Most of us see mental illness as something in which a person walks around naked and lives in a cemetery, speaking gibberish to everyone she meets. Most mentally ill people do not live in cemeteries! So, do not look in the cemetery for a mental patient. A mentally ill woman may be living in your bedroom with you. Some of the most famous missionaries who changed the face of Christianity were married to *"The Patient."*

William Carey, the famous missionary to India, married when he was only nineteen years old. He married a woman who was six years older than he was. His wife struggled with a certain kind of mental illness for many years, accusing him of many outrageous things over the years. In spite of this difficult marriage, he was able to accomplish great things for God.

There are a wide range of conditions that are considered to be mental illnesses. Only a trained eye can notice and diagnose these conditions. Mental illness is very much like bad behaviour. The bad behaviour of the person stems out of the mental pressure under which the person labours. Women are more prone to certain mental illnesses than men. Always remember that mental illness can present itself as bad behaviour.

The Beast: A Woman with Undiagnosed Mental Illness

A Christian leader, who had been married to his beautiful and gentle wife for several years, began to contemplate divorcing his wife. This was because she was behaving very badly, accusing him of many evils. She had become impossible to live with and was constantly in a confrontation with him and his mother. It seemed as though she just hated her husband's mother. Finally, he decided to leave his wife. He was certain that he would divorce her.

Before he could go ahead with the divorce, his wife attacked him physically. He defended himself as his wife physically assaulted him. Whilst she was attacking him, it occurred to him that his wife was behaving very abnormally. Right there in their home, for the first time in his life, it occurred to him that his wife could have a mental illness.

Even though he was a medical person, it had never occurred to him that his wife could have a mental illness. Being a good Christian brother, he decided not to divorce his wife but rather get treatment for her. Indeed, it became clear as time went on, that his wife was truly labouring under a real mental illness. She was admitted to the hospital shortly after that and had to go through several bouts of treatment.

This story illustrates the fact that many people are actually suffering from mental illness. In this case, the mental illness manifested as bad behaviour towards her mother-in-law.

The Beast: A Woman with Depression

We use the terms anxiety and depression casually, but they are actually specific medical diagnoses.

What is depression? When a pastor's wife is depressed, she may have a very low mood, a loss of interest in life, and an inability to experience pleasure in activities that she once enjoyed.

This mood change may manifest as sadness or irritability. When a lady is depressed, she may lose weight. Some ladies put on weight when they are depressed. Depressed women may wake up very early; find it difficult to go to sleep, lying in bed for hours.

Indeed, such a depressed woman may be difficult to live with. The man of God may overreact in response to his chronically moody, unhappy and accusative wife.

Accusations and discontentment are symptoms of depression. Women suffering from "anxiety" or "depression" can also come up with symptoms such as general weakness, bodily pains and tiredness. These symptoms are often not clear enough to allow a doctor to make a definitive diagnosis. A depressed person may always seem to be unwell with one problem or another, constantly seeing the doctor. Some of the symptoms of illness may be so serious that extensive investigations are carried out to locate the source of the pain and to investigate the specific dangerous sounding symptoms that are put forth by the patient.

After several attempts to treat different illnesses, it may begin to occur to the doctors that they are dealing with a mental illness.

Mental illness may lead to very bad behaviour and very unpleasant marriage problems. These problems, because of their chronic nature, can even lead to separation or divorce.

The ability to diagnose depression in a wife is very important. The proper diagnosis will help you to have compassion on your wife. With the proper diagnosis and treatment, you will have the grace to carry on with your marriage.

The Beast: A Woman with Anxiety

Anxiety is a treatable psychiatric condition that many pastors' wives have.

Amazingly, anxiety can have specific physical effects such as an increased blood pressure and increased heart rate. A person with anxiety has a sense of dread or panic.

People with anxiety disorders can have various symptoms that may seem as real as anything. For instance people with anxiety attacks may have chest pains and think they are having a heart attack. They may also feel that any pain they have in their head is as a result of a tumour. Women with anxiety are fearful, tense, irritable, restless, watching and waiting for signs of danger. Such people also have bad dreams, nightmares and are filled with the fear of dying or the fear of a loved one dying.

As you can see, these psychiatric symptoms could be applied to many people that you know. Indeed, many ordinary people walking around actually need a bit of psychiatric care.

The Beast: A Woman with a Personality Disorder

Personality disorders occur when people exhibit behaviour that deviates markedly from what you would expect based on an individual's culture and background. Personality disorders affect the person's personality, life and existence. *People with personality disorders are inflexible and unable to change their patterns and behaviour in spite of counselling and help offered.*

Indeed, what a psychiatrist may call a personality disorder, a pastor may call stubbornness and disobedience to the Word of God. Indeed, there are several personality disorders that afflict and affect people that we know. A pastor or his wife could easily suffer from a personality disorder.

1. A lady with a *Paranoid Personality Disorder* has a pattern of mistrust and suspicion. Simply put, people with this disorder have a tendency to be sensitive, easily offended, guarded and suspicious.

2. A lady with a *Schizoid Personality Disorder* has a tendency towards a solitary lifestyle, secretiveness, emotional coldness and sexual apathy. She is detached from social relationships and has a restricted range of emotional expression.

3. A lady with a *Schizotypal Personality Disorder* has a need for social isolation. When a person has this kind of personality disorder, she displays odd behaviour in thinking and often holds unconventional beliefs. A person like this may have a poor rapport with others and tend to withdraw. Such a person is cold, unemotional and aloof. People may find her eccentric or peculiar.

4. A lady with an *Antisocial Personality Disorder* fails to conform to the law and repeatedly performs acts that could lead to his or her arrest. Deception, lying, irritability and

aggressiveness are symptoms of this personality disorder. She may have repeated physical fights with others without regard for her own safety or that of others.

5. A lady with a *Borderline Personality Disorder* is unable to maintain interpersonal relationships. She will be insecure and have an unstable self-image and a poor sense of worth. She is likely to give herself to promiscuous sex and have eating disorders. Recurrent suicidal behaviour and self-injuring behaviour are also symptoms of this condition. Princess Diana was suspected of having this condition.

6. A lady with a *Histrionic Personality Disorder* shows excessive emotionality and attention seeking. She displays seductive behaviour and inappropriate dressing because she is seeking attention. Such people are lively, dramatic, enthusiastic and flirtatious. Such a lady may show an exaggerated display of emotions such as hugging someone she has just met or crying uncontrollably during a sad movie. Such people go through frequent job changes and become easily bored and frustrated. People with histrionic personality disorders therefore have numerous relationships.

7. A lady with a *Narcissistic Personality Disorder.* This type of person is preoccupied with power, prestige and vanity. You would easily describe such a person as self-centred. This type of woman pursues only selfish goals and is obsessed with herself. Such a woman will take advantage of others, always trying to exaggerate her own importance, achievements and talents. In her childhood, she may have received excessive praise for her good behaviour. She grew up requiring constant attention and admiration.

8. A lady with an *Avoidant Personality Disorder.* This is a lady who is hypersensitive to criticism and extremely sensitive to any negative comment or remark. She undergoes self-imposed social isolation. This means that she is shy, anxious and avoids physical contact because of her feelings of low self esteem. Such people also have a strong inferiority complex and are therefore difficult to relate with.

9. A lady with a *Dependent Personality Disorder* is a very submissive person who exhibits clinging behaviour. She always seems to have an excessive need to be taken care of. Such a person has difficulty in taking everyday decisions unless she has a lot of advice and reassurance from others. Such a person can easily be taken advantage of by men because she always needs someone to assume responsibility for the major areas of her life. Indeed, she cannot initiate projects and lacks the drive and energy for them.

10. A lady with an *Obsessive-Compulsive Personality Disorder* is preoccupied with orderliness, perfectionism and control. A person with this disorder can pay attention to so many minute details and facts that this perfectionism would actually prevent the timely completion of tasks. This kind of person is also rigid and inflexible in her beliefs. Someone who is preoccupied with details, rules, lists, order and organization will be difficult to work with because of her unpleasant rigidity and stubbornness.

Indeed, such people are also unduly preoccupied with productivity and fruitfulness to the exclusion of pleasure and interpersonal relationships.

I am sure that all of you who have read this list of personality disorders have found yourself in there somewhere. You will realise that most of us have personalities that can shift easily into the realm of a "disorder". Often, when there is a mental illness of any sort, people spiritualise their misbehaviour, refuse the medical diagnosis and subsequently refuse counsel or treatment.

The Beast: A Woman with Bipolar Disorder

Some pastors are married to women with a bipolar disorder. You can understand the disease by understanding the word, 'bipolar'. Bipolar speaks of two poles or two extremes. On one hand, the beautiful princess may be a calm, gentle, sweet and well-behaved hostess impressing the outside world with her charm. On the other hand, she may be violent, angry and uncontrollable.

When the other extreme sets in, such a woman may go on spending sprees or engage in behaviour that is abnormal, such as taking drugs, alcohol or even becoming aggressive.

One day, a great man of God's wife ran through the house removing all the cutlery from the house because she believed an evil spirit was in the house. She then walked for miles with the children, covering them with a towel because she believed that the moon-god wanted to strike them. You can imagine the confusion in the pastor's home as he saw this abnormal behaviour and hyperactivity in an apparently normal person. Later on, this unstable woman surprised everyone with an announcement that she was divorcing her husband.

These bouts of hysterical uncontrollable behaviour, along with depressed moods, show the picture of the bi-polar syndrome.

Behold, we have two people in one!

Indeed, even the trained eye finds it difficult to diagnose some of these diseases. There are many doctors who cannot pick out mental illnesses. In such cases, the man of God and his children could be harmed by the wife who, in a moment of hysteria and violence, could inflict harm on the family.

One day, a man of God was sitting at a table with a medical doctor. The medical doctor knew the man of God and his family quite well. The doctor let out a bombshell that surprised the man of God. He said to him, "I think your wife has the bipolar mental illness." The man of God was taken aback and asked, "Are you trying to say that my wife is a mental patient?"

Indeed, the entire family struggled to accept the diagnosis. You see, it is not easy to accept the reality that a seemingly normal person is actually mentally ill.

The Beast: A Woman with Schizophrenia

Some pastors are married to women with Schizophrenia. Schizophrenia is an unfortunate illness in which a person actually goes mad. Schizophrenic patients experience hallucinations in which they hear voices, have bizarre delusions and disorganized thinking and speech. Their bizarre thinking pattern leads them to speak in sentences that are not connected in meaning. Their speech is sometimes described as a "word salad".

There was once a pastor of a very large church in a prominent city. He lived on the twenty-fourth floor of a high-rise apartment block. His marriage suffered terribly due to a developing mental illness in his wife. No one could understand the conflicts and problems that the pastor seemed to be beset with (nobody usually understands).

No one expected what was going to happen next. One day, whilst the pastor was away at work, his wife took two of her three children and threw them out of the window of their apartment complex. Both children died when they hit the ground. The third child was able to escape from her wild mother in the house.

Indeed, it was only after this violent episode that the family and the congregation realised that the pastor's wife was actually mad. Before this incident, everyone thought the pastor had a bad marriage and did not love his wife. After this episode, the mentally ill wife was confined to a mental institution. A few years later, the pastor remarried amidst even more criticism. Was it right for him to marry when his wife was permanently mentally ill? Should he have remained unmarried and waited for her healing? A good question!

The Beast: A Woman with a Delusional Disorder

Many pastors are married to women with delusional disorders. A delusional disorder is a condition in which a person has a fixed delusion. Apart from this particular delusion, there are no other symptoms of mental illness in the person. A delusion is something one believes in, in spite of contrary evidence. The type of disorder that a woman with delusional disorder has is what we call a "non-bizarre delusion.'

A bizarre delusion is a belief that is incredible, out of this world and virtually impossible. A person who has a belief that the ceiling is about to drop on his head has a bizarre delusion.

A non-bizarre delusion is a belief that is plausible, possible and even likely. A person who has a belief that her husband is having an affair with his old girlfriend is having a non-bizarre delusion. It is non-bizarre because it is believable, it is possible and it may even be likely.

Indeed, some pastors are married to women with delusional disorders. I spoke to a lady who had a devoted husband. Her marriage was breaking down because she was constantly accusing him of being interested in another lady.

Somehow, I knew for sure that her husband was not having an affair with the lady. His wife was accusing her husband of having an affair with a virgin who was about to get married.

I asked her, "Do you think your husband is having an affair?"

She said, "Yes, I do."

I asked again, "Do you think your husband is committing adultery with this virgin lady who is about to get married?"

She answered, "I do."

I asked yet again, "Do you actually believe that your husband is having sexual intercourse with this virgin?"

She said, "I do. He is having sex with her and I know it."

No matter what I said, I could not convince this lady that she was believing the wrong thing and destroying her marriage. She maintained her stand, thereby reducing her marriage to a mere social co-existence.

This lady could easily have a delusional disorder because she had no other mental symptoms. She simply had one *non-bizarre delusion*, which she stuck to for many years, no matter what was said or done.

When you accuse a person of doing something that he is not doing, you greatly affect the relationship between yourself and the person. Marriages are changed forever when accusations begin.

John Wesley's wife was a difficult person to live with. In fact, it was not possible to stay with her. Her mind was filled with the conviction that John Wesley was having affairs with other women. One day, she told John Wesley,

"DESIST FROM RUNNING AFTER STRANGE WOMEN FOR YOUR CHARACTER IS AT STAKE"

Mrs Molly Wesley

Some people said that the kindest way to look at her was to think of her as having had a mental illness.

John Wesley said of her, **"IT WOULD TAKE MORE THAN A THOUSAND YEARS FOR HER TO UNDO THE MISCHIEF SHE HAS DONE TO ME"**.

A sign of mental illness is the lack of insight, where the person is not aware of what she is doing. Even though Mrs Wesley mistreated her husband greatly, on her deathbed, she left him a ring as a token saying,

"I DIE IN LOVE AND FRIENDSHIP TOWARDS HIM."

Mrs Wesley

It is possible that Mrs Wesley never comprehended the extent of hurt and damage that she caused John Wesley by her behaviour. That is a clear sign of a *Patient*. A mental patient often has *no insight*. A *Patient* cannot grasp what she is doing and the effect it has. When you recognize this lack of insight, you are far more able to have compassion for the *Patient*.

CHAPTER 28

What it Means to be Married to *A Combo*

S ome people get married to a person who is a combination of many things. She may be a combination of a *Wild Cat*, a *Prison Officer*, a *Quarrelsome Queen* and the *Uncaring Independent.*

The Combo: A Quarrelsome Queen

The husband of the *"Combo"* has many issues in his marriage. He tries to address them, deal with them, handle them and negotiate with her for years but he still does not win her love.

In this kind of marriage the husband suffers terribly and deeply. Every single issue that comes up in the marriage is not simply between man and wife but between man, wife, mother- in-law and sisters-in-law. There is nothing like a private issue between husband and wife. No argument with this wife is simply an argument with her. Every argument becomes an argument with her, her parents and her siblings. When there is an issue that builds up tension in the house, the tension is between husband, wife and the wife's entire family. The husband is always criticized and compared to her younger sister's husband who is a politician. This is constantly done by her mother and sister, and very often in the presence of the husband's family.

In this marriage, the husband is made to feel that nothing he ever does is good. He tries to be supportive as a husband but absolutely nothing is appreciated. He would pay money for her to further her education. This will never be appreciated – he is rather told that he is not supportive.

He would even sell his car to get her a better car but it is still not appreciated and she would complain that he has bought her an old car. He can leave her in charge of all his money and never question what she uses it for but it is still regarded as nothing.

The Combo: The Accuser

Every night as soon as this husband falls asleep, the *Combo* would take his phone and go through all his messages. She, like John Wesley's wife, would copy them, forward them to others, delete some of the messages and even respond to some of the messages. When the aspersions are in full bloom, the phone searching comes on every single night.

The Combo: A Poor Performer

If you are married to such a *Combo*, there is almost never food in the house.

The husband who is married to a *Combo* is ALWAYS buying food or one thing or the other but never having food made for him at home. This husband exists on a diet of readymade noodles or readymade rice that has to be bought and brought home! He NEVER has food at home.

Amazingly, the *Combo* turns out to be a dirty person. Pots with food can sit in the kitchen for over a week. If you opened the pots, you would find putrefied, rotten food turned into liquid with very thick mould over it. Pots sit in the kitchen for over a month unwashed, until the "A1" husband decides to wash them himself. Hundreds of sachets of water that are used to cook or do other things in the house will sit in the kitchen on the sink, counter, floor and everywhere. HUNDREDS of plastic bags cover the floor. Sometimes, thick dust covers the floor and water drops make the kitchen muddy and filthy.

Unfortunately for the "A1" husband, dirty laundry are left in the washing basket for over three months and sometimes six months. Believe it or not, some of these husbands sometimes throw away clothes that have become awfully mouldy.

Sometimes, half washed boxer shorts and singlets are left in a bucket in the bathroom for three months - till the water turns black.

Mattresses and pillows and other beddings that are taken out for airing never return to the house for months and months and months. Everything is simply left outside by this non-performing *Combo*.

The Combo: A Wild Cat

When married to a quarrelling queen *Combo*, there are endless arguments. You will never be able to communicate and say "Let's sit down and discuss like adults and address an issue. Let us try to simply address our problems." Such discussions end up in tantrums, shouting and quarrelling. The *Combo* would go off in a huff and you would wonder if she is mentally stable. She will break things, throw things against the wall, destroy things, cry and try to hurt herself with sharp objects. Nothing the husband ever says to her is listened to. Every time there is a quarrel, she screams and shouts and cries and wails for the whole house to hear. The husband is constantly humiliated, disgraced, embarrassed, reduced to nothing in front of her family.

The Dangers

The husband who does not handle the pressures well may begin to masturbate and watch pornography. He starts making new friends to keep him company and cheer himself up. Her behaviour pushes him away and pushes him into a place he never thought he could be. He will try to talk with her but she will keep mocking him and accusing him.

At the end of a work season, when everyone is eager to go home, the husband remains silent because he is so afraid of going back home. Sometimes, during a trip away from home, the "A1" husband is unable to sleep when the thoughts of returning home come to him. He is so worried and afraid as he keeps wondering what would happen when he gets home. The journey home is often terrible, filled with anxiety, fear and dread.

He feels like a devil in his own house. One day, a nice "A1" husband was pushed to the wall and said to his wife, "I will kill you!" He had been pushed to the point of hatred.

OVERCOMING IN MINISTRY AND MARRIAGE

CHAPTER 29

Overcome in Your Marriage by Fighting to Survive

FIGHT THE GOOD FIGHT of faith, lay hold on eternal life, whereunto thou art also called, and hast professed a good profession before many witnesses.

1 Timothy 6:12

Y ou must fight to gain control and bear fruit in your short life on this earth. Few of us can live in this world without getting married. Most of us need marriage and need women in our lives. To say that marriage will help your ministry is to over-simplify things. The written Scriptures reveal many negative things about marriage and women that should scare any Christian. Marriage can be more of an extra war than a form of help.

Marriage will help your ministry, but marriage will also introduce certain problems and conflicts into your life. Without marriage, you will also be subject to another group of problems. Where there are no oxen, stables and rooms are very clean. Once you have cows, you are going to have the problem of cleaning up your surroundings.

Where no oxen are, the crib is clean: but much increase is by the strength of the ox.

Proverbs 14:4

Choosing to marry is to choose the kind of problem you want to have. It is going to be either this problem or that problem. You must gain the upper hand in the marriage experience so that you can fulfil your calling.

A declaration of war must be made. You must accept that you are at war because you are married. Accept that your marriage may be a section of the war you are called to fight. You will have to learn new survival strategies. You will have to develop ways to adapt and to live as a warrior. Instead of enjoying a soft life of ease, pleasure and satisfaction, your marriage may simply be war.

Once you are married you are stuck! She is stuck to you and you are stuck to her! You have to stay with what you've got! You have to fight and you have to survive without becoming bitter, immoral or divorced. Can you overcome? Can you survive? Yes, you can and yes, you will!

Accept the fact that you may have entered into a war by getting into marriage. Satan wants to use your marriage to turn you into a phantom of what you were actually called to be. Many married people do not fulfil their calling or their ministries. Many married pastors are phantoms of what they were really called to be.

Fight the "spirit of the phantom"! There is a devil that wants to use your marriage to turn you into a phantom of yourself. Satan wants you to become a fraction of what you were born to be.

Satan's plan is to destroy you through your marriage. Through the problems of your marriage, satan intends to lead you to the spirit of fornication, adultery, bitterness and hatred. This is the strategy to turn you into a phantom. You must do any and everything not to become irrelevant in ministry through divorce. Identify the spirit of fornication that is sent to turn you into a phantom in ministry. You must do any and everything not to become irrelevant in ministry through marriage.

Identify the spirit of bitterness that is sent to fight against you. Do not allow bitterness to turn you into a phantom. Bitterness will change your spirit and make you cynical and angry. Therefore you must do anything and everything to forgive your spouse. Otherwise, you will become irrelevant in ministry. Declare that you will walk in forgiveness and that you will love whomever God has given you!

You must overcome discouragement! Take consolation in the fact that you are not alone. Most of the things that you experience are also being experienced by others. Know that women can be used as weapons of war. You are a winner! You are more than a conqueror! Your destiny is clear! You have overcome in every situation!

CHAPTER 30

Overcome in Marriage by Blocking Five Specific Attacks

Satan has a long term plan to destroy you. You must believe and understand that there is an intelligent demon orchestrating events in your life. Your marriage is being destroyed and your life is being destroyed by an intelligent creature who is manipulating events. You must realise that there are five end points which satan is trying to bring you to. Once you are aware of these five destinations, you must fight them specifically and block them absolutely.

Five Things to Fight Specifically and Block Absolutely

1. Specifically fight against Satan's plan to make you into a man with two wives.

A bishop then must be blameless, THE HUSBAND OF ONE WIFE, vigilant, sober, of good behaviour, given to hospitality, apt to teach;

1 Timothy 3:2

Does anyone want to be a bishop? Does anyone want to be a Christian leader? Does anyone want to be a pastor? The famous condition for this job is that you must be the husband of one wife (1 Timothy 3:2). Satan therefore is trying hard to make you become the husband of *more* than one wife!

You do not only become a husband of two or more wives through polygamy. Take care, because you can become the husband of more than one wife through a *bad marriage*, through *a separation* or through *a divorce*. Any of these three events can lead you to have additional relationships and marriages in your lifetime. Most ministers start out with a vision of being a husband of one wife.

What would make you become the husband of more than one wife? How does that happen to a man of God? Whenever a relationship fails, a door is opened for a new one. Through the bad experiences of your marriage, you may be forced to develop relationships with more than one woman.

Although you set out to be the husband of one wife, the circumstances you encounter in marriage may cause you to deviate from your original and ideal vision. This is what has happened to many people who were very committed to marriage and to the things of God.

Many have ended up with more than one wife and more than one marriage. Some of them ended up divorcing and remarrying whilst some of them just added on a relationship or two!

Through the wisdom in this book, you will be delivered from the traps and snares that seek to turn you into the husband of more than one wife.

2. ***Specifically fight against Satan's plan to make you cultivate unhealthy friendships and relationships with the opposite sex.***

Because of your difficult marriage, you can develop amazing relationships and friendships. You may just start enjoying the conversations and chats with very friendly members of the other sex. Soon you will be going to watch films with these other ladies and buying ice cream for them. You may later on find yourself visiting the homes of such people and becoming close to them. Although such a relationship may not actually progress into adultery, you may soon have all kinds of inappropriate relationships and friendships. This is one of satan's plans for your life. It is your duty to reject the development of inappropriate and ill-defined relationships with ladies.

3. *Specifically fight against Satan's plan to turn you into an adulterer.*

It is your duty to resist walking on that road to destruction. As a sexually starved husband, you may meet delightful, eager, young girls. You will be attracted to them because they are much more cheerful and appreciative of you than your " angry headmistress" wife. It is your duty to reject this walk into adultery. God is showing you the long-term plan of satan for your life. Simply reject and avoid all such friendships and relationships before they become a temptation and a test in your life.

4. *Specifically fight against Satan's plan to lead you into internet-based sexual relationships.*

Through the internet, you can have almost anything you want. As a love-starved, sex-starved husband, it is no surprise that the internet becomes the source of love and sex. Through computers, websites and phones, you may soon develop the ability to "satisfy" yourself through the internet. This is one of the aims of satan for your life. Since you know that this is one of the devils' dark plans for you, it is your duty to directly resist walking onto that road to destruction.

5. *Specifically fight against Satan's plan to make you violent and if possible, a murderer.*

Through bitterness and hatred, you may grow to dislike your spouse very much. You may slap, hit and beat up your wife. You may hold her by the neck and strangle her to death before you know what you have done. There are many people in prison today who killed their own wives. Whenever there is a death of a married man or woman, the first person to be accused is his spouse. Hatred easily builds up in a marriage. Be careful of this long-term plan of satan for your life. Satan wants to destroy you.

CHAPTER 31

Overcome in Marriage by Blocking Out the Possibility of Divorce

Thus saith the Lord, Stand ye in the ways, and see, and ASK FOR THE OLD PATHS, where is the good way, and walk therein, and ye shall find rest for your souls. But they said, we will not walk therein.

Jeremiah 6:16

The Master Key to Staying Married for Life

What is the master key to staying married for life? The master key is to ask for the old paths! You can reduce your chance of getting divorced by behaving like the fathers and mothers of yesteryear.

In the olden days, the idea of being divorced was completely out of the question. That is the foundation upon which marriages lasted entire lifetimes. Once upon a time, there was no option of ever leaving a marriage. Everyone settled down and tried to make the best of the situation.

Modern marriages have greatly increased their chances of experiencing divorce by contemplating divorce as an option. Wipe divorce out of your mind completely. Do not even consider it as an option! When it is not an option, it will stop occurring to you to divorce every time you have a big problem at home. Decide to have one of the olden day marriages where divorce was completely unheard of and never considered as a possibility!

A young lady once told her mother that she wanted to divorce. Her mother's reply was simple. She said, "I will not advise you to divorce because I come from an era where we fixed things that were spoilt."

She continued, "In my time, when something was spoilt, we did not throw it away and just get a new one. We fixed it!"

It is time to go back to the old paths where we stop throwing spoilt marriages away.

It is time to go back to the old paths where we repair things that are spoilt.

The old paths are the master key to staying married for a lifetime! Our fathers were somehow able to survive. We will survive too as we walk down the old paths of righteousness and self-sacrifice. Receive grace! Receive wisdom! God is helping you!

Thus saith the Lord, Stand ye in the ways, and see, and ASK FOR THE OLD PATHS, where is the good way, and walk therein, and ye shall find rest for your souls. But they said, we will not walk therein.

Jeremiah 6:16

CHAPTER 32

Overcome in Marriage by Hard Decisions

Wherefore if thy hand or thy foot offend thee, cut them off, and cast them from thee: IT IS BETTER FOR THEE to enter into life halt or maimed, rather than having two hands or two feet to be cast into everlasting fire. And if thine eye offend thee, pluck it out, and cast it from thee: IT IS BETTER FOR THEE to enter into life with one eye, rather than having two eyes to be cast into hell fire.

Matthew 18:8-9

Jesus gave a great word of wisdom when He said, "It is better to cut off your arm and enter into heaven." It is a bad thing to go to heaven without one of your arms. But it is worse to go to hell with two arms. Jesus Christ was teaching us about how to take decisions when we are faced with two bad options.

Hard Decisions to Take: Choosing Between Two Bad Options

You must always take the better of the two bad options. Many ministers are often faced with two bad options: sometimes, both options you are faced with are biblically sound. Sometimes, both options you face do not have a clear biblical backing.

Let us look at a few examples of hard decisions that Christian marriages are often faced with.

Separation is a bad option but it may be better than living in strife, confusion and fruitlessness.

Separation is a bad option but may be better than fighting each other, abusing each other and living in a constant state of quarrelling, strife, unhappiness, tension and stress.

Separation is a bad option but may be better than fighting physically as a couple and embarrassing yourselves in public.

Crushing your wife's spirit and subduing her absolutely, is a bad option but it is better than allowing a *Wild Cat* to torment you.

Accepting to suffer is a bad option but may be better than saying goodbye to your life partner and never seeing each other again.

Suffering in marriage is a bad option but may be better than never getting married and becoming a homosexual.

Ignoring your spouse is a bad option but may be better than fighting all the time.

Living together and just tolerating each other's existence is a bad option but may be a difficult choice you have to take instead of separating.

To live with someone you don't love is a bad option but may be a difficult choice you have to take instead of divorcing.

Ignoring your wife is a bad option but it may be a better choice than withdrawing your love for her and treating her like one of your servants.

Separation is a bad option but may be a difficult choice you have to make, instead of growing in hatred for each other as you live together.

Separation is a bad option but may be a difficult choice you have to make, instead of dying prematurely because of marital quarrels.

Completely ignoring your spouse is a bad option for your marriage and life, but may be a difficult choice you have to take instead of becoming a murderer.

Divorce and remarriage is a bad option but may be better than becoming a murderer

Divorce and remarriage is a bad option but may be better than becoming an adulterer.

To separate from each other and live in different rooms is a bad option but may be a difficult choice you have to make instead of divorcing.

To separate from each other and live in different houses is a bad option but may be a difficult choice you have to make instead of divorcing.

To separate from each other and live in different cities is a bad option but may be a difficult choice you have to make instead of divorcing.

To separate from each other and live in different countries is a bad option but may be a difficult choice you have to make instead of divorcing.

Unfortunately, like most normal human beings on this earth, you may one day be faced with the need to decide between two *bad options*. That is what it means to choose between a rock and a hard place.

In marriage, you may have to choose one of these bad options I have described above.

No one can take that decision for you! No one can decide certain things for you! You have to decide which bad option you are going to take and trust that you are taking the right decision. You may have to choose between living in continuous strife or living in separate houses! You may have to decide between living in separate countries or fighting with each other constantly. You may have to decide between living in separate cities or tolerating each other's existence for the rest of your lives.

When it is time for exams, no one can do them for you. You have to work out the equation yourself based on what you know. Your wisdom will be seen by the results you get in the examination. This life is an examination! Your wisdom will be seen by the decisions you take based on the options you have. Remember that God will judge you for everything you decide.

Jesus our Saviour, decided never to get married or to have a wedding! Wisdom is justified of her children. We will find out everything we do not know when we get to heaven.

CHAPTER 33

Overcome in Your Marriage by the Power of a Mordecai

Esther had not yet shewed her kindred nor her people; as Mordecai had charged her: for ESTHER DID THE COMMANDMENT OF MORDECAI, LIKE AS WHEN SHE WAS BROUGHT UP WITH HIM.

Esther 2:20

The presence of a Mordecai is the presence of a trainer, a coach, a teacher, a pastor or a father!

Even if you attend classes for one year to understand marriage, you may not really understand what you are being told. You may read a thousand books about marriage and still not understand. You need to experience marriage to really understand what it is.

To have a good marriage, every lady needs to have a Mordecai in her life. Mordecai's involvement in the marriage of Queen Esther is a revelation that must be understood by those who love marriage and want it to work.

Esther was the replacement for a stubborn and difficult-to-control woman called Vashti. Vashti vaunted herself and opposed her husband, the king. *She lost her position and her marriage and was replaced by an orphan.* This fantastic occurrence serves as a warning from history. You cannot dwell proudly with your man! You must understand how to comport yourself as a wife who is submitted to and secondary to her husband and his leadership.

The difference between Vashti and Esther is that Vashti did not have someone to tell her what to do. If she had had a Mordecai, he would have told her, "It will not harm you to put on your best dress and parade in front of those guests."

Mordecai would have said to her, "If you were not the king's wife, you would consider it a great honour if he called for you."

It is important to realise that marriage is so complicated that no girl will come into marriage knowing already what to do and how to behave. Also, most girls receive only a percentage of the complete training they actually need for marriage.

Many girls make fatally deficient decisions about how to behave in marriage. They continue to make these mistakes until their marriages are beyond repair. When the marriage eventually breaks down, it is blamed on the man because he is the easiest target for the blame game. Men are seen as senseless and insensitive animals, who just follow their desires for the next enticing female.

A sister was told by her mother, "When a man's wife dies, he will, by all means, have a new woman in his life before six months are over. As for men, they are animals!"

Such comments only reveal a negative attitude towards men.

The reality is that many girls have a dream to marry without understanding what it really means. They dream about their wedding day and the excitement of being with a man. However, the reality of the mundane chores and duties they will have to perform is lost on them. It is almost impossible for an unspiritual woman to understand how to relate to a real man.

This is where a Mordecai comes in! Esther trusted Mordecai and continued to follow his instructions on how to behave in the king's palace, long after she was married. A Mordecai is someone who gives instructions that only help a marriage become better and stronger!

Esther had not yet shewed her kindred nor her people; as Mordecai had charged her: for ESTHER DID THE COMMANDMENT OF MORDECAI, LIKE AS WHEN SHE WAS BROUGHT UP WITH HIM.

Esther 2:20

A good and humble wife needs counsel over a long period time, until she is mature enough to know what to do. The Bible teaches that the older women can teach the younger women.

THE AGED WOMEN likewise, that they be in behaviour as becometh holiness, not false accusers, not given to much wine, teachers of good things; THAT THEY MAY TEACH THE YOUNG WOMEN to be sober, to love their husbands, to love their children,

Titus 2:3-4

It is obvious from this scripture that the younger women are completely ignorant on how to behave. The scripture is telling us that older women are to teach young women how to love their husbands.

Obviously, the young women do not know *how to love a husband.* They may know how to have a boyfriend. They may know how to have sex in the nightclubs, on the beach and in their boyfriend's car. They may know how to dress up, do their hair and their nails, but they may not have a clue about how to love a husband.

Many younger Christian wives have bad attitudes towards sex. However, as they get older, they understand the importance of love and change their attitudes. Sadly, that change sometimes comes too late to save the happiness in the marriage. It is obvious that the older women have learnt much more about what marriage is. The presence of a Mordecai is the presence of a trainer, a coach, a teacher, a pastor or a father. Mordecai will help you to know what to do!

Some ladies do not have a Mordecai because they are stubborn and they do not obey anyone, not even their fathers, their uncles, pastors and other God-given teachers. Don't marry someone who does not have a Mordecai in her life. You will probably be marrying a difficult case and you will be called *'the brother who has that difficult wife'.*

If your beloved does not have a Mordecai, don't blame anyone if you are distressed in the years to come!

CHAPTER 34

Overcome in Your Marriage by the Wisdom of Naomi

Then Naomi her mother in law said unto her, my daughter, shall I not seek rest for thee, that it may be well with thee? And now is not Boaz of our kindred, with whose maidens thou wast? Behold, he winnoweth barley to night in the threshingfloor. Wash thyself therefore, and anoint thee, and put thy raiment upon thee, and get thee down to the floor: but make not thyself known unto the man, until he shall have done eating and drinking. And it shall be, when he lieth down, that thou shalt mark the place where he shall lie, and thou shalt go in, and uncover his feet, and lay thee down; and he will tell thee what thou shalt do.

And she said unto her, all that thou sayest unto me I will do.

Ruth 3:1-5

Naomi is symbolic of the woman who understands a man and has the humility that is required to be married. Naomi gave Ruth the keys she needed to win the heart of Boaz. Naomi told Ruth exactly how to win Boaz's favour and get his attention. Naomi was an older woman and she knew much more about how to behave towards a man. Naomi was the right person to teach Ruth what to do. It is always a blessing when an older woman teaches a younger woman.

Perhaps this is why older men often marry older women instead of going for fresh young maidens, just out of school. She may be fresh and exciting but void of wisdom. She may be fresh and exciting but lacking training. Naomi was there to impart wisdom to Ruth. May you have a 'Naomi' who will help you in your marriage!

THE AGED WOMEN likewise, that they be in behaviour as becometh holiness, not false accusers, not given to much wine, teachers of good things; THAT THEY MAY TEACH THE YOUNG WOMEN ...

Titus 2:3-4

Naomi's Seven Steps

Naomi gave Ruth seven steps to follow. Ruth obeyed each one of them and had a successful relationship with Boaz. These are her seven steps.

1. **Young lady, choose the man that I choose for you.**

   Then Naomi her mother in law said unto her, my daughter, SHALL I NOT SEEK REST FOR THEE, that it may be well with thee?
   And NOW IS NOT BOAZ OF OUR KINDRED, with whose maidens thou wast? Behold, he winnoweth barley to night in the threshing floor.

   Ruth 3:1-2

Naomi sought rest for Ruth. Naomi sought out something good for her daughter-in-law. Naomi chose Boaz for Ruth and Ruth accepted it. Ruth did not say that Boaz was an old, unexciting man. Many people want to choose for themselves. Choosing for yourself at a certain stage of your life can be very tricky. Perhaps, choosing for yourself at a time when you do not understand the issues at stake is the basis for most failed marriages. Because Naomi chose a husband for Ruth, she had a successful marriage.

2. Young lady, wash yourself and be a clean person.

WASH THYSELF therefore, and anoint thee, and put thy raiment upon thee, and get thee down to the floor: but make not thyself known unto the man, until he shall have done eating and drinking.

Ruth 3:3

Some ladies are not clean. It may surprise you that some ladies do not like bathing. Some ladies have smells and odours they are not even aware of. Naomi, an experienced woman, knew that being clean and washed was very important for an older man. Perhaps young men, in their excitement, would not notice certain smells. But Naomi knew that Ruth needed to be clean if she was to succeed. That is why she told Ruth, "Wash thyself".

3. Young lady, anoint and improve yourself!

Wash thyself therefore, and ANOINT THEE, and put thy raiment upon thee, and get thee down to the floor: but make not thyself known unto the man, until he shall have done eating and drinking.

Ruth 3:3

After washing herself, Naomi wanted Ruth to anoint herself for her man. Naomi wanted Ruth to smell nice to Boaz. She wanted Ruth to enhance her beauty and look very attractive to Boaz. It is important to enhance your beauty, make yourself look attractive and be nice. You may think it is natural for a woman to want to look nice to her husband. Unfortunately, many women just want to look nice in public but not to the man who sees them mostly in private. You will be shocked to see what many of the stunning beauties you know look like at home. At home, the jewellery is taken off and the artificial additions are removed! The beautiful dresses are off! At home, many of the fashionable ladies you see in public are hairless, sweaty, smelly and all dressed up in rags.

4. **Young lady, wear the right clothes.**

   Wash thyself therefore, and anoint thee, and PUT THY RAIMENT UPON THEE, and get thee down to the floor: but make not thyself known unto the man, until he shall have done eating and drinking.

   Ruth 3:3

   Naomi wanted Ruth to wear the right clothes that would make her look more beautiful when Boaz saw her. Some people only look nice at weddings and when going out. But it is also important to look nice at home and in every casual setting.

5. **Young lady, understand the man you are married to.**

   Wash thyself therefore, and anoint thee, and put thy raiment upon thee, and get thee down to the floor: but MAKE NOT THYSELF KNOWN UNTO THE MAN, UNTIL HE SHALL HAVE DONE EATING AND DRINKING.
   And it shall be, when he lieth down, that thou shalt mark the place where he shall lie, and thou shalt go in, and uncover his feet, and lay thee down; and he will tell thee what thou shalt do.

   Ruth 3:3-4

   A woman is very different from a man. Without training, a woman will never know how to behave towards a man. I am sure the same can be said of men. Without training, a man will never understand a woman. How wonderful it is when an experienced woman teaches the younger lady how to relate to her man!

6. **Young lady, do not push the man around.**

    Wash thyself therefore, and anoint thee, and put thy raiment upon thee, and get thee down to the floor: but make not thyself known unto the man, until he shall have done eating and drinking.

    And it shall be, when he lieth down, that thou shalt mark the place where he shall lie, and thou shalt go in, and uncover his feet, and LAY THEE DOWN; AND HE WILL TELL THEE WHAT THOU SHALT DO.

    Ruth 3:3-4

    God created the man to be the head. God created the woman to submit to the man. This is the natural and divine order. Every time a woman tries to push a man around, there are problems. You can get your man to do what you want without forcing him around.

    Naomi knew that it was important to approach Boaz gently, humbly and submissively. A younger woman may not know how important that is. But the older woman certainly knew this truth! This is why the counsel of Naomi was so important. This is why the teaching of an older woman is critical for a successful marriage.

7. **Young lady, choose a marriage that will give you rest.**

    And he said, Blessed be thou of the Lord, my daughter: for thou hast shewed more kindness in the latter end than at the beginning, inasmuch as THOU FOLLOWEDST NOT YOUNG MEN, whether poor or rich.

    Ruth 3:10

    Naomi chose the kind of marriage that would give rest to Ruth. Ruth may have chosen the kind of man that would impress the world. Ruth could have chosen a young man who was more handsome and not pot-bellied.

It was the fact that she was interested in the old man, Boaz, that really touched his heart. Boaz commented on the fact that she was not looking for a rich young man. Most girls would simply like to marry a rich young man. Naomi's advice guided Ruth away from following after riches and youthfulness and into the will of God. Only an older woman would advise this young lady to go for the older man, Boaz.

CHAPTER 35

Overcome in Marriage by Separation

And the fruit of righteousness is sown in peace of them that make peace.

James 3:18

This chapter reveals that *"separation"* is the ancient wisdom that many have used to achieve peace. You must know and believe that peace is essential for fruitfulness. As a spiritual person, you must understand the importance of peace. The wisdom of apostle James is clear. No peace, no fruit!

No one has borne fruit without peace. The scripture is very clear on how important peace is for fruitfulness. Because David was fighting all the time, he could not build the temple of God. God did not want him to touch the temple because of his continuous conflicts.

If you want God to use you to build His church, you must achieve peace at all costs. A large percentage of conflicts in ministry are actually marital conflicts. Do not be upset because you have to fight for peace! You are just like many other ministers! Do not believe the "perfect marriage picture" that most ministers put out. They look all smiley and beautiful but there are many conflicts beneath the waters.

Be a spiritual person and accept the reality that peace is something you have to fight for in order to bear fruit.

It is sad to say that you may have to separate from your spouse in order to live peacefully. I hope this never happens to you but it is a reality that we have to talk about.

There are times that separation from your spouse is the only way for you to achieve peace, so that you can work for God. In this kind of separation, you do not divorce or legally dissolve the marriage. You just separate your lives so that you can have peace and exist on earth.

In the separation I am speaking about, you part company with your spouse and live separately. In this separation, you do not formally divorce your spouse. In this separation, you do not marry anyone else nor have sexual relations with any other person. In this separation, you live apart in different houses, cities or countries and endure a life of loneliness in order to bear fruit for the Lord. In this kind of separation, you may visit each other when you feel like it or simply pay a courtesy call. In this kind of separation, you do not live in hatred of each other but in peace. In this kind of separation, you have more time to fellowship with the Lord. Please be aware that there are temptations associated with this kind of "separation arrangement". However, this "separation arrangement" may be better than living together and killing each other in the process.

1. **Separate from your spouse like Abraham separated from Lot and experienced peace.**

   And Abram said unto Lot, Let there be no strife, I pray thee, between me and thee, and between my herdmen and thy herdmen; for we be brethren.

   Is not the whole land before thee? SEPARATE THYSELF, I PRAY THEE, FROM ME: if thou wilt take the left hand, then I will go to the right; or if thou depart to the right hand, then I will go to the left.

   Genesis 13:8-9

There are times a marriage can be compared to the partnership that existed between Abraham and Lot. The wisdom of Abraham for your marriage is the wisdom of separating yourself from someone who brings conflict into your life. Abraham separated his life from the life of Lot because he knew that living with Lot was bringing too much conflict and strife. He knew that strife would not help him to become the father of many nations. God had promised to multiply Abraham exceedingly. God has also promised to multiply your ministry exceedingly.

You must accept that you cannot live peacefully with everyone. Sometimes, you have to go your separate ways and love each other from afar. Many married couples are actually happier when they do not live together. Knowing each other from afar, calling each other often and missing each other may make you a happier person. Abraham's reason for having conflict with Lot was because the land could no longer contain the two of them.

Abraham separated from his nephew because the land could no longer carry them or keep them together.

"And the land was not able to bear them, that they might dwell together: for their substance was great, so that they could not dwell together" (Genesis 13:6). One of the meanings in Hebrew of the phrase, "The land could no longer bear them" is "the land could no longer *marry* them".

Sometimes, couples are unable to live together in a single room. There are times they will do better in two separate rooms. There are times they will do better in two separate houses. There are times they will do better in two separate countries.

After Abraham separated from Lot, *he became more fruitful* and still had great love for Lot. "And the Lord said unto Abram, after that Lot was separated from him, Lift up now thine eyes, and look from the place where thou art northward, and southward, and eastward, and westward: for all the land which thou seest, to thee will I give it, and to thy seed for ever. And I will make thy seed as the dust of the earth: so that if a man can number the dust of the earth, then shall thy seed also be numbered" (Genesis 13:14-16).

When Lot got into trouble, Abraham gathered together an army and fought for Lot.

If continuous strife is destroying you, your marriage is comparable to the situation of Abraham and Lot. The wisdom that Abraham had then was to love his nephew from afar. The wisdom of Abraham in this matter is to love each other by moving away from dwelling together in the same space. Abraham's wisdom for peace was to live separate lives contentedly and happily.

2. Separate from your spouse like Isaac separated from Abimelech and experienced peace.

And Abimelech said unto Isaac, GO FROM US; for thou art much mightier than we.

Genesis 26:16

Isaac followed the wisdom of his father, Abraham. He knew that he had been called to be fruitful. Every time he dug a well, there was conflict. He knew that he could not bear fruit and fulfil the will of God with that amount of conflict. Isaac kept moving away from those who brought him conflict. Perhaps your marriage is giving you a lot of conflict and you will never be able to bear fruit because of it.

Isaac dug a well and he thought he was going to have a great time enjoying the well he had laboured for. But to his amazement there was only conflict. He called that well Esek.

And Isaac's servants digged in the valley, and found there a well of springing water. And the herdmen of Gerar did strive with Isaac's herdmen, saying, The water is ours: and he called the name of the well ESEK; because they strove with him.

Genesis 26:19-20

Then he dug another well. There again, he thought he was going to have the time of his life. But it was not to be so. There was only conflict. He called that well *Sitnah* and moved on.

And they digged another well, and strove for that also: and he called the name of it SITNAH.

Genesis 26:21

On his third try, there was no conflict. There, he found peace and he called the place Rehoboth. He said, God was going to make him fruitful because there was now room for fruitfulness.

And he removed from thence, and digged another well; and for that they strove not: and he called the name of it REHOBOTH; and he said, For now the Lord hath made room for us, and we shall be fruitful in the land.

Genesis 26:22

Dear friend, you need room and peace so that you can be fruitful. You cannot be fruitful with the kind of conflict that you are experiencing everyday. Spouses have to learn to leave each other to do their own thing so that they can have peace in their lives.

3. Separate from your spouse like John Wesley separated from his wife and experienced peace.

The great founder, John Wesley, separated from his quarrelsome wife and never attempted to marry anyone else. Through the separation, he achieved the peace he needed to have for the work of God.

If ever the founder John Wesley had grounds for depression, one at least was the unfortunate breakdown of his marriage to Molly. She stole or burned his papers and constantly criticized him in conversation to others. But in 1771, she left without warning and went to live in Newcastle for three years.

John Wesley, the founder, tried to humour her and took her on his travels but never understood her troubled spirit. He assumed that her lies about his actions and character were an attempt to vindicate her own. He believed her to be a woman of true faith but of poor judgment. Sometimes, he wondered whether she had married him for his money derived from his books, only to find out that his fortunes were not for his own use.

John Wesley and his wife were separated for good, at a point. She left him finally and set up a home with her son. In 1777, John Wesley accidentally met his wife, Molly, who said she was willing to return home. John Wesley agreed, provided that she restored his documents and took no more.

On reflection, he wrote to withdraw his offer for them to be reunited because it would seem to be an admission that he had been guilty of all her accusations. He wrote to her and said, "For instance, you have said over and over that I have lived in adultery for the past twenty years." She had lied to others that he had had an affair with Sarah Ryan, the housekeeper at Bristol. She had also claimed that Sally, Charles Wesley's happy and devoted wife was his mistress (girlfriend).

John Wesley wrote to his wife, "Do you believe this or do you not? If you do, how can you think of living with such a monster?"

It seems that she made another approach to come back and live together with John Wesley. But in 1778, John Wesley wrote an uncompromising letter to her and said, "You have laid innumerable stumbling blocks in the way of the wise and the unwise. You have served the cause and increased the number of rebels and atheists. You have weakened the hands of those that love and fear God.

If you were to live to a thousand years twice told, you could not undo the mischief which you have done. And until you have done all you can towards it, I BID YOU FAREWELL."

As you can see from John Wesley's words, he was quite resolute about not being together with his wife. He was implementing the wisdom of separation to its uttermost. John Wesley never met his wife again. When John Wesley's wife died in 1781, he was not told of her death for several days, nor the place and hour of her funeral.

4. Separate from your spouse like Kathryn Khulman separated from her husband and experienced peace.

It was after Kathryn Khulman separated from her husband that her ministry developed into the worldwide healing ministry she is known for. She never attempted to marry again.

There are many couples that should be separated for their own good. They should live apart and not live in the same house. Sometimes they should not even live in the same city or the same state for their own sake.

Certain men of God will have a greater peace of mind if they are separated from a brawling woman or a contentious woman.

This separation I am speaking of, involves separation without having another woman on the side or creating another family but returning to the former level of loneliness you were in before you got married. John Wesley is the best example of this kind of separation. He separated from his wife and carried on with ministry till the very end of his life.

This kind of separation is a very positive thing for the purpose of accomplishing great things in ministry. Kathryn Khulman is another example of someone who separated from her spouse in order to accomplish great things with her life. She did not marry anyone else, nor did she have any affair with anyone.

CHAPTER 36

Overcome in Marriage by Acceptance and Suffering

For unto you it is given in the behalf of Christ, not only to believe on him, but ALSO TO SUFFER for his sake

Philippians 1:29

When thou passest through the waters, I WILL BE WITH THEE; and through the rivers, they shall not overflow thee: WHEN THOU WALKEST THROUGH THE FIRE, thou shalt not be burned; neither shall the flame kindle upon thee.

Isaiah 43:2

That which is crooked cannot be made straight: and that which is wanting cannot be numbered.

Ecclesiastes 1:15

The ancient wisdom of Solomon is that you cannot straighten a crooked thing. How true that is! Many things will never change. You will find out for yourself. You will have to calm down and accept many ugly things that you cannot change.

Jacob never intended to marry two women. He never intended to have two relationships. Through no fault of his, he was forced into a second relationship that he had not bargained for. In the end, this second relationship with Leah, which he had never wanted, was used by God to fulfil the destiny of Israel.

We will not have perfect lives. We are often being deceived about many things in this life. When you discover you have been deceived as Jacob was, you must make the most of your situation and move on. Accept the fact that you have made mistakes and accept the fact that your life may work out in an imperfect way.

Like Jacob, Accept Your Spouse Even Though You Have Been Deceived

Jacob accepted that he would have two women, even though he had planned for one. He accepted that he would stay married to someone he did not really love. He accepted the fact that he could not set aside Leah after marrying her.

Many people want to set aside their partners when they realise they have been deceived. It is not right for you to set aside your marriage when you discover that you have made a mistake. Most people make mistakes about their marriages. Most people do not know much about marriage when they are entering into it. Most people regret marrying their partners at one point or the other. They may not admit it but it is the truth.

The wisdom of Jacob is to accept the lopsided, odd, unfortunate and inappropriate marriage you have found yourself in and limp with it through this life, so that you can please God.

You may, indeed find yourself marrying twice, or even three times. I am sure you never intended to. You are just like Jacob who never intended to have two wives in one lifetime. Do not allow your failure to prevent you from being fruitful. Sometimes, God chooses the point of failure to make you fruitful.

God chose Leah, the unfortunate and unloved mistake of Jacob's life to bring forth His will. It was Leah, who bore most of Jacob's twelve children. Rachel, the loved one, only had two children. God used Bathsheba, the mistake of David's life, to bring forth Solomon the wise man. None of his legitimate wives could bring forth such a son. What a shock! You must trust God to right the wrongs of your life. You must trust God to help you weave your way forward.

CHAPTER 37

Overcome in Your Marriage By the Wisdom of Paul

And lest I should be exalted above measure through the abundance of the revelations, THERE WAS GIVEN TO ME A THORN IN THE FLESH, the messenger of Satan to buffet me, lest I should be exalted above measure.

For this thing I besought the Lord thrice, that it might depart from me.

And he said unto me, My grace is sufficient for thee: for my strength is made perfect in weakness. Most gladly therefore will I rather glory in my infirmities, that the power of Christ may rest upon me.

Therefore I TAKE PLEASURE IN INFIRMITIES, IN REPROACHES, IN NECESSITIES, IN PERSECUTIONS, IN DISTRESSES for Christ's sake: for when I am weak, then am I strong.

2 Corinthians 12:7-10

There are several ways you could look at your marriage. One of the ways to think of your marriage is to see it as a *"thorn in the flesh"*.

You could see your marriage as a *reversible mistake* that you have made!

You could also see your marriage as an *irreversible mistake* that you have made!

You could see your marriage as *God's gift* of comfort to you!

You could also see your marriage as God's way of *testing your character.*

No one knows exactly what Paul's *"thorn"* was. It could have been anything. It could have been a sickness, a mistake, a financial crisis, an old friend, an old problem, a secret sin, a curse or even a relationship. One of the things it could also have been was a difficult marriage had he been married.

Whatever the "thorn" was, it really affected Paul. He was unable to get rid of this problem. That sounds like someone's marriage! You can easily get rid of an employee you do not want. You can easily get rid of a disloyal associate you do not want. But you cannot easily get rid of your marriage.

Perhaps, if Paul were married, God's grace to him would have been to allow him to suffer through marriage. Whatever the "thorn" was, it was a powerfully humbling experience to the great apostle. Many people are humbled greatly by their marriages.

What it Means to Accept a "Thorn in the Flesh" Marriage

1. **Accepting a "thorn in the flesh" is to accept something from God Himself.**

If your marriage is a "thorn in the flesh", it is something that has been given to you by God. It is not right or even possible to get rid of this "thorn in the flesh". If you divorce or remarry you are likely to have another buffeting agent released against you.

Paul said that a messenger of satan had been given to torment him. A demon that has been allowed by God is the only demon that you cannot bind. God Himself has allowed the demon to be continually present in your life.

If God blesses your ministry, you must expect a "thorn in the flesh" as a necessary humbling agent. If it happened to Paul, why can it not happen to you? I cannot tell if your marriage will be a "thorn in the flesh", but I can say that some people's marriages are *"thorns in the flesh"*!

John Wesley admitted that if he had had a good marriage like his brother Charles, he would probably not have travelled around, doing the work of ministry like he did. A thorn was given to him in the form of his wife, Molly. A thorn keeps you perked upright! A thorn keeps you on your toes! A thorn keeps you from relaxing!

2. **Accepting a "thorn in the flesh" is to accept that your marriage will be a weak spot in your life.**

Apostle Paul said, *"Therefore I take pleasure in infirmities."*

That is what it means to accept a thorn in your flesh. If your marriage is a "thorn in the flesh", you must receive it as *an infirmity and a weakness* in your life. It is a weakness that you cannot get rid of. It will always be a weak point that satan will attack.

Your marriage will be a weakness that you must live with. It is like having a sickness you must take medicine for every day.

3. **Accepting a "thorn in the flesh" is to accept a reproach.**

Apostle Paul said, *"I take pleasure in reproaches."*

If your marriage is a "thorn in the flesh", you must receive it as a reproach that God has allowed to be with you. Indeed, it will be a reproach that you cannot get rid of. It is something you must live with.

A reproach is an embarrassing aspect of your life. Some marriages are a great embarrassment to the man of God. There are many men of God who are embarrassed by the kind of woman they have ended up with. She is unspiritual and not complementary at all to his ministry. That is a reproach!

Such a wife can bring shame as people question the wisdom that the man of God used in selecting such a person. I remember a pastor whose wife would drink alcohol at programmes where he ministered. He was continuously embarrassed by his drunken wife. She would make things worse by drinking her alcohol with her sleeping medicine and anti-depressant drugs that had been prescribed to her. One day, after taking her medicines and her alcohol, she just died in her bed.

4. Accepting a "thorn in the flesh" is to accept that you will be in need even though you are married.

Apostle Paul said, *"Therefore I take pleasure in necessities."*

If your marriage is a "thorn in the flesh", you must see it as God allowing you to have a need. Paul said, "I take pleasure in necessities."

If you have a "thorn in the flesh" marriage, you will always be in *need* of love, you will always be in need of comfort, you will always be in *need* of peace, you will always be in *need* of sex, you will always be in *need* of food, you will always be in *need* of support and you will always be in *need* of care. That is what it means to have a thorn in your flesh.

With such a marriage, you will see others having their needs met, whilst you live in deprivation. Take heart, dear friend, there are many men that have many needs, even though they are married.

5. Accepting a "thorn in the flesh" is to accept that you will be persecuted through your marriage.

Apostle Paul said, *"Therefore I take pleasure in persecutions."*

If your marriage is a thorn in the flesh, you must accept it as a kind of *persecution* that comes to a righteous man. Perhaps you are not suffering the persecution of being martyred for Christ, but you may suffer persecution from your own darling "beast".

You may not have a wicked Roman Emperor like Nero or Caligula breathing persecution down your neck. Your own wife will suffice! She will make up for the absence of the wicked Roman tyrants. The problems the early Christians had from Roman tyrants cannot be repeated in the world today. Through marriage, you may experience an equivalent level of suffering. If you survive that sort of marriage, in heaven, you may sit next to Christians who were killed by gladiators, lions and Roman soldiers.

People will wonder what you are doing sitting next to such heroes. All you will say is you were married to Samantha for thirty-three years and when you came to heaven you were ushered to sit amongst these heroes.

One pastor spoke about his marriage. He said, "If I am able to stay married till I die, it will be an achievement that is equivalent to all the souls won by Billy Graham!"

6. Accepting a "thorn in the flesh" is to accept that your marriage will distress you.

Apostle Paul said, *"I take pleasure in distresses."*

Your marriage may be a *distressing situation* that God has chosen for you to experience. You will often be perplexed in marriage! You will be amazed and you will also be distressed throughout your marriage.

Your distressing marriage is not something you can end by going to court. It is a spiritual thing that has been given to you to experience. It is a demon that has been given access to you for a spiritual reason.

Arise and be strong. Pray for grace to lead you on! *"T'was grace that brought us safe thus far; and grace will lead us home!"*[1]

Notice men of God that look stressed and distressed. Much of that stress comes from the troubles at home.

---

[1] *"Amazing Grace"*, John Newton (1779).

CHAPTER 38

Overcome in Your Marriage by Receiving the Prophetic Message of Your Marriage

The beginning of the word of the Lord by Hosea. And the Lord said to Hosea, GO, TAKE UNTO THEE A WIFE OF WHOREDOMS and children of whoredoms: for the land hath committed great whoredom, departing from the Lord.

Hosea 1:2

Hosea's unfortunate marriage brought out a strong message from God. A marriage can give you a message from God. You can receive the spirit of understanding through your marriage experiences. Having a difficult wife may be God's way of giving you His message. If you have a bad or difficult marriage, you may be walking in the footsteps of the prophet Hosea. Hosea is the man of God who ended up being married to an unfaithful prostitute. You may be married to a *Loveless Oldie* or a *Quarrelsome Queen*. It is just a variation of what Hosea had. Do not be sad if you have a terrible experience in your marriage. Welcome to the "Hosea Club of Difficult Marriages"!

The nature of your marriage and the experiences you have can constitute a message from God to you. The experience Hosea had in marrying a prostitute became a message to him from God. God speaks to the man of God through his marriage. Perhaps, the reason why you have experienced all that you have is to help you receive a message from God.

Hosea was shown what God thinks about people who run after other gods. The marriage experience with a prostitute caused Hosea to learn what it was like for God when His children run after other gods.

Things God Can Teach You through Your Marriage Experience

And the Lord said unto him, Call his name Jezreel; for yet a little while, and I will avenge the blood of Jezreel upon the house of Jehu, and will cause to cease the kingdom of the house of Israel.

Hosea 1:4

And she conceived again, and bare a daughter. And God said unto him, Call her name Loruhamah: for I

**will no more have mercy upon the house of Israel; but
I will utterly take them away.**

Hosea 1:6

God may allow you to have a certain kind of marriage so
that He can give you a certain message through the marriage
experience. He made Hosea marry a prostitute so that He could
give him certain messages.

There are prophetic messages that God can cause you
to receive by causing you to enter a marriage that has certain
characteristics. The characteristics of your marriage may be a
clear prophetic message from the Lord for you. Many people
have misunderstood Hosea. They have felt that God made Hosea
marry a prostitute to have children with odd names.

The big surprise for you today is that God may have sent you
to marry an equally problematic person for precisely the same
reason that He made Hosea marry a prostitute. Your marriage
may be as mysterious as Hosea's marriage and the purpose of
your marriage may be as mysterious as Hosea's.

Many pastors have wondered whether God guided them into
their marriages. "If God guided me, why would I end up with a
prostitute or a clearly deficient woman?"

God guides those who ask Him to guide them. Instead of
thinking of your marriage as a mistake, think of it as a prophetic
message! Acknowledge the Lord in all thy ways and He shall
direct thy paths. Once you acknowledged the Lord before you
got married, God has directed your paths.

You may have married a man who slaps women. You may
wonder why you should marry a "slapper" after all the prayers
you have prayed.

You may wonder why you would marry a *Quarrelsome
Queen* after all the prayers you offered up. You may wonder why
you should marry a loveless person after all the love you give.

These are experiences that give you a deep understanding of God and His word. Perhaps you are just like Hosea and have entered a strange marriage with a prophetic message for your life and ministry. Let us have a look at some of the mysterious messages God may be giving you through your marriage.

1. **God could cause you to be married to a man who does not provide for you so that you will not take for granted His provision in many ways.** This is to send a message to you to look up to God and stop looking to man for provision.

   For she did not know that I GAVE HER CORN, AND WINE, AND OIL, and multiplied her silver and gold, WHICH THEY PREPARED FOR BAAL. Therefore will I return, and take away my corn in the time thereof, and my wine in the season thereof, and will recover my wool and my flax given to cover her nakedness.

   Hosea 2:8-9

2. **God could make you marry someone who does not love you very much so that you understand what the Lord experiences when His children do not love Him.** In such a marriage, you would pour your love out in vain just as God has poured out His love on us in vain.

   Through this experience, you discover the importance of the scripture, "You must love the Lord your God with all your heart, and with all your mind and with all your soul."

   And thou shalt love the Lord thy God with all thy heart, and with all thy soul, and with all thy mind, and with all thy strength: this is the first commandment.

   Mark 12:30

   Instead of loving the Lord with all your mind and all your soul, you have loved a woman with all your mind, and all your heart and all your soul. What a mistake! You have given to a human being what you should have given to God!

You have sown seeds of love into the wrong place and you have received a painful reward for that mistake. Through your marriage, God may be directing you to love the Lord God with all your heart, soul and might.

And the Lord direct your hearts into the love of God, and into the patient waiting for Christ.

2 Thessalonians 3:5

3. **God could make you marry a man or woman who accuses you constantly so you understand the power of the accuser of the brethren.** In this kind of marriage, you would learn and understand all about accusations and how the accuser of the brethren functions. You will understand why satan is called the "accuser of the brethren". Most people do not understand that title. To most Christians, accusations sound like a nuisance rather than a real problem.

You may not fully understand the word "accuser" but when you experience it in marriage, you will get the full revelation of the work of the devil and of demons. Through your marriage to an accuser, you will fully understand the work of satan in the church. As you experience division and separation in your marriage, you will develop a deep understanding of how division and separation occur in a church through accusation. As love, happiness and peace are destroyed in your marriage, you will understand the power of accusation. You will understand how love, happiness and peace are destroyed in churches through false and baseless accusations. These are things you may never understand until you experience a real and a living accuser next to you.

Then he showed me Joshua the high priest standing before the angel of the Lord, and Satan standing at his right hand to accuse him. The Lord said to Satan, " The Lord rebuke you, Satan! Indeed, the Lord who has chosen Jerusalem rebuke you! Is this not a brand plucked from the fire?

Zechariah 3:1-2 (NASB)

4. **You could be married to someone who cannot have a child. God may give you this experience to reveal to you the importance of bearing fruit.** Perhaps, God is giving you the spirit of understanding through your marriage. There are levels of understanding that you cannot attain by reading a book. You will learn the truth about barrenness through your experience of marriage. You will discover how God yearns for His children to bring forth fruits that abide.

Now will I sing to my wellbeloved a song of my beloved touching his vineyard. My wellbeloved hath a vineyard in a very fruitful hill:

And he fenced it, and gathered out the stones thereof, and planted it with the choicest vine, and built a tower in the midst of it, and also made a winepress therein: and he looked that it should bring forth grapes, and it brought forth wild grapes.

And now, O inhabitants of Jerusalem, and men of Judah, judge, I pray you, betwixt me and my vineyard.

What could have been done more to my vineyard, that I have not done in it? Wherefore, when I looked that it should bring forth grapes, brought it forth wild grapes?

And now go to; I will tell you what I will do to my vineyard: I will take away the hedge thereof, and it shall be eaten up; and break down the wall thereof, and it shall be trodden down.

Isaiah 5:1-5

5. **God could make you experience the death of your spouse so that you would understand that everything on earth is vain indeed.** Perhaps you have not really believed or understood how vain and useless earthly ventures truly are. Everything here is temporary. Marriage is a temporary arrangement! Children are temporary tenants! Human love is transient! Your buildings are vain attempts to create eternal dwellings. Your gardens are a phantom of the eternal "Gardens of Eden" that we look forward to.

But perhaps you have not believed all these things. Most people do not believe the scripture. Many Christians do not believe the Bible at all. Solomon said it all!

Vanity of vanities, saith the Preacher, vanity of vanities; all is vanity. What profit hath a man of all his labour which he taketh under the sun?

Ecclesiastes 1:2-3

The death of the spouse whom you really love will send a strong message of the futility of life into your soul. You will receive a deep understanding of the phrase, "Vanity of vanities!" You tried to make a home! You tried to have love! You tried to live in peace! And it all blew up in your face! You are left with futility, sorrow, depression and memories that are difficult to erase. Through the futility of the death of your spouse, you will understand the need to set your affection on things above and not on things below. Indeed, God will deliver into your heart one of the strongest messages of wisdom and understanding, through the death of your spouse.

Set your affection on things above, not on things on the earth.

Colossians 3:2

6. **God could make you experience the bitter and wicked character of your angelic looking wife so that you will understand that there is none righteous, no not one.** Perhaps, you did not believe there was none righteous. But through your marriage you will understand that no human being is perfect or righteous. Every time your angelic wife, whom everybody praises, treats you badly, you will understand the scripture even more. You will marvel at how people are deceived and impressed by your "nice" and "angelic" wife. You will understand how the whole world lies in wickedness and deception.

As it is written, "There is none righteous, not even one…"

Romans 3:10 (NASB)

7. **God could give you a rebellious son so that you would learn and understand the message of the prodigal son.** You will discover what God is experiencing from us as we rebel and go far from Him. You will understand what it is like to bring up a child who turns against you. You will understand what it is like to have a child who does not want to be near his father.

And he said, a certain man had two sons: and the younger of them said to his father, Father, give me the portion of goods that falleth to me. And he divided unto them his living. And not many days after the younger son gathered all together, and took his journey into a far country, and there wasted his substance with riotous living

Luke 15:11-13

CHAPTER 39

Why Some Pastors Are Divorced

Some Pharisees came to Jesus, testing Him and asking, "IS IT LAWFUL FOR A MAN TO DIVORCE his wife for any reason at all?" And He answered and said, "Have you not read that He who created them from the beginning made them male and female, and said, ' For this reason A man shall leave his father and mother and be joined to his wife, and the two shall become one flesh'? So they are no longer two, but one flesh. What therefore God has joined together, let no man separate." They said to Him, " Why then did Moses command to give her A certificate of divorce and send her away?" He said to them, "Because of your hardness of heart Moses permitted you to divorce your wives; but from the beginning it has not been this way. And I say to you, WHOEVER DIVORCES HIS WIFE, EXCEPT FOR IMMORALITY, AND MARRIES ANOTHER WOMAN COMMITS ADULTERY." The disciples said to Him, "If the relationship of the man with his wife is like this, it is better not to marry.

Matthew 19:3-10 (NASB)

There are many reasons for getting divorced. Some people do have a biblical basis for their divorces and it is important to know the reasons why some people do enter into divorce.

Some people get divorced because they just want a new woman. There are men who have a bad character and mistreat their wives. Indeed, such people may end up divorced. There are also men who are multiple adulterers and really do not have what it takes to be married to one woman.

There are also people who want a pretext for divorcing their wives. They cook up reasons for divorcing their wives. Be careful! Don't you know that you will stand before God and be judged in everything you do?

And I saw the dead, small and great, STAND BEFORE GOD; and the books were opened: and another book was opened, which is the book of life: and THE DEAD WERE JUDGED out of those things which were written in the books, ACCORDING TO THEIR WORKS.

Revelation 20:12

But those are not the type of people I am talking about in this chapter.

In this chapter, I am talking about men of God who are not adulterers and who have no intention of ever divorcing but find themselves getting divorced! There are many people who have had to divorce in spite of their resolve never to do so.

It is important not to crucify the good and the bad together on the same tree. Jesus was crucified together with thieves. Righteous Jesus was given the same treatment as wicked criminals! That is wrong and also dangerous. Not all situations are the same.

So here is why some men and women do get divorced in spite of their determination never to do so.

When a minister's marriage breaks down, you will hear a very common storyline.

The usual story is that there is a lovely, gentle, humble and faithful wife who has been dwelling happily and peacefully with her man of God. This humble faithful wife of the man of God is an innocent sufferer and has become a victim of a terrible evil. There is an evil woman who is hunting for the man of God and she is luring and enticing him. This humble faithful wife of the man of God is married to a husband who cannot control himself as he helplessly follows his banal desires. The man of God is an almost mad, senseless and impulsive man when it comes to this other woman and does not seem to like his own beautiful wife any more. The man of God seems to be helplessly overcome by a wicked female who has been lurking in the background for a long time.

The man of God who was serving God, suddenly becomes disobedient and no longer follows the will of God and begins to act like someone who is possessed and out of his mind. The man of God then abandons his lovely, gentle and faithful woman who could harm no one. The man of God is unfeeling and does not care about his family any more and moves out of the house to have fun with a new, exciting and strange woman. It is easy to paste a man with the accusation of being unfaithful. Men are well known to desire numerous women. It is, therefore, not bizarre to suggest that a pastor is sleeping with someone else.

This is the usual storyline. However, there are cases in which this stereotyped story is not true. There are many cases in which the husband is *not* unfaithful. Indeed, statistics show that a very low percentage of pastors have affairs with other women.

Remember the scripture that says "judge with righteous judgment." Do not lump all divorces together and give them one and the same judgment. In this chapter I want you to know some reasons why some pastors are divorced.

Reasons Why Some Pastors are Divorced

1. Some men of God have wives *who commit adultery with other men* and this becomes the reason for their divorce.

Some men of God *do not* have affairs with other women but are accused as though they did.

And Potiphar's wife soon began to look at him lustfully. "COME AND SLEEP WITH ME," SHE DEMANDED.

Genesis 39:7 (NLT)

Some good men of God get divorced because they are married to unfaithful wives. Amazingly, there are quite a number of wives who are not faithful to their men of God. Jesus was clear that adultery and immorality are a good reason for getting divorced. There are many pastors who are accused of leaving their wives for other women whereas it is in fact the other way round.

Some Pharisees came to Jesus, testing Him and asking, " IS IT LAWFUL FOR A MAN TO DIVORCE his wife for any reason at all?" And He answered and said, "Have you not read that He who created them from the beginning made them male and female, and said, 'For this reason A man shall leave his father and mother and be joined to his wife, and the two shall become one flesh'? So they are no longer two, but one flesh. What therefore God has joined together, let no man separate." They said to Him, " Why then did Moses command to give her A certificate of divorce and send her away?" He said to them, "Because of your hardness of heart Moses permitted you to divorce your wives; but from the beginning it has not been this way. And I say to you, WHOEVER DIVORCES HIS WIFE, EXCEPT FOR IMMORALITY, AND MARRIES ANOTHER WOMAN COMMITS ADULTERY."

The disciples said to Him, "If the relationship of the man with his wife is like this, it is better not to marry."

Matthew 19:3-10 (NASB)

Can I divorce? Is it right to divorce my wife? Jesus answered this question clearly. Jesus was asked this very question and He answered it fully. The answer that Jesus gave is all the answer you need about whether it is right or not to divorce the "beast" in your life. The Scripture above is clear and needs no interpretation. It will amaze you to know that many husbands who have adulterous wives simply do not speak about it and simply do not react to their wives having affairs. They just carry on living with them as though nothing happened.

2. Some people are divorced because *they believe they are in a situation that is similar to God divorcing Israel.*

And I saw, when for all the causes whereby backsliding Israel committed adultery I HAD PUT HER AWAY, AND GIVEN HER A BILL OF DIVORCE; yet her treacherous sister Judah feared not, but went and played the harlot also.

Jeremiah 3:8

God has declared Himself to be a divorcee because He could not stand the behaviour of His bride Jerusalem. Both Jeremiah and Isaiah knew that God had divorced Israel His love.

No one will ever be able to tell you clearly that it is right to divorce your wife.

God knows every circumstance and you will be judged for doing the right or wrong thing. If you think I am going to tell you that it is right to divorce, then you might as well stop reading. I can only show you what the scripture says about God divorcing and leave you to walk by your own faith. God told us in His word not to divorce. But he Himself has divorced Israel whom He loved.

Thus saith the Lord, Where is the bill of YOUR MOTHER'S DIVORCEMENT, WHOM I HAVE PUT AWAY? Or which of my creditors is it to whom I have sold you? Behold, for your iniquities have ye sold yourselves, and for your transgressions is your MOTHER PUT AWAY.

Isaiah 50:1

You will never have everyone agreeing with one opinion on a divorce or a marriage. Whatever you do, some people will think you were right and some will think you were wrong. Even with the choosing of a wife, some people will think you are right and some will think you are wrong.

God, in His righteousness decided to set aside His bride. Even though God in His righteousness decided to get a divorce, you as a pastor will always be unsure of yourself when it comes to divorce.

You will always be unsure of what the Christian community really thinks about you. You cannot tell whether they will trust your decision to separate from your wife. If you divorce, you will always be despised by a section of the Christian community. There are those who believe that it is always wrong to divorce no matter what.

If you divorce, you will always have a kind of "limp" in the ministry.

If you divorce, you will never be sure whether you were at fault or not.

If you divorce, you will need to have great faith to walk on in full view of the public.

Marriage or divorce is an act of your faith and your wisdom. Unfortunately it is an act you carry out in the full view of the world. The faith you act out will be judged by the Lord in heaven. The wisdom you act out by divorcing will play out on earth. It is in heaven that you will eventually be justified or condemned for getting divorced.

3. Some men of God are divorced because *they are married to a "beast"* and can no longer dwell together with her.

They prefer to dwell in the wilderness than to continue for one more day in the house with this woman.

It is BETTER TO DWELL IN THE WILDERNESS, than with a contentious and an angry woman.

Proverbs 21:19

If you have ever been behind the scenes when ministry marriages break up, you will often hear another version of Christian marriage.

You will often hear about the "beasts" in the woman that the man endured for many years.

You may hear about a wife who stopped cooking for her husband or serving him food for many years.

You may hear about a wife who lives in another house or in another country against her husband's wishes, leaving him to have affairs with other women if he wants to.

You may hear about a wife who had affairs that the husband forgave and ignored.

You may hear about the behaviour of a wild and angry wife who tormented her husband with her wild uncontrollable behaviour for many years.

You may hear about stubbornness of the highest order.

You may hear about a marriage in which there was no sex for many years.

You may hear about a man who has had to masturbate to relieve himself of his sexual needs because his wife was unwilling to have sex with him.

You may hear about a man who watches pornography in order to have some excitement since his wife has no interest in sex at all.

263

You may find out that the husband has had girlfriends on the side because his wife was unwilling and uncaring about sex.

You may hear about how the husband has tried to castrate himself in order to deal with his unmet sexual desires.

You may hear about a domineering wife who controls her husband as if he were her little boy or servant.

You may hear about a wife who has manifested clear psychiatric symptoms for years.

You may hear about a wife who has had personality disorders for many years.

You may hear about a marriage in which the man was accused incessantly about many things he had never done.

You may hear about a sweet relationship that was destroyed because of continuous and complicated accusations.

You may hear about a man who is both the father and the mother to the children because the mother simply refuses to do her work as a mother.

You may hear about a man who caters for his children, cooks for them, baths them, dresses them up and does homework with them, whilst his wife never lifts a finger to look after the children she brought forth.

You may hear about a woman who was drinking alcohol regularly and embarrassing her husband by getting drunk in public.

You may hear about a woman who was using so much money that she caused financial crises in her home.

You may hear about a man who is known in every restaurant in the city because he never has food at home!

You may even hear about a wife who physically beats up her husband!

If you do bother to find out more, you will find out that the marriages of ministers are much more complicated than they seem on the outside. The breakup of pastors' marriages may be far more complicated than they seem.

This is why you cannot prescribe one solution for all marriages. You must not be like the herbalist who has one potion for all problems. You must be a minister of God's Word and walk in righteousness, justice and equity. You must be fair and true to God and to all the sides of the equation.

4. **Some men of God are divorced because** *they feel they can handle the reaction* **of the Christian community to their divorce.**

Who art thou that judgest another man's servant? to his own master he standeth or falleth. Yea, he shall be holden up: for God is able to make him stand.

Romans 14:4

There are people who believe that God's judgment is the basis of their standing or falling. They have decided that they stand or fall before God and man's opinion does not matter anymore. They no longer care who judges them. It is the Lord's opinion of them that matters to them.

It is also important to note that adultery is the reason that Jesus gave for a man to legally leave his wife. Jesus said, "But I say unto you, that whosoever looketh on a woman to lust after her hath committed adultery with her already in his heart" (Matthew 5:28).

According to this scripture, if you look at a woman lustfully you have already committed adultery. Most men have looked upon a woman with lust and therefore most men have committed adultery and therefore most women are scripturally entitled to a divorce.

However, if you divorce, you will find yourself in a very "grey area". Some people will support you if you divorce but you will also be criticised by many others. There will always be different opinions about your decision to divorce. I have observed many different attitudes and reactions from Christians towards divorce.

Some people believe that your marriage is your own business and they therefore have no comment to make about your decision to divorce.

Some people simply take sides, depending on whom they are closer to.

Some people always believe that the man is wrong, no matter what.

Some people will no longer follow you because you are divorced.

Some people will follow you no matter how many times you marry or divorce.

Some people believe strongly in never divorcing no matter the occasion.

Some people believe in having polygamous marriages like the patriarchs in the Bible.

Some people believe strongly in endless counselling to resolve the unresolvable.

Some people believe in taking radical decisions about marriage.

Some people believe strongly in divorcing if there is a need to.

Some people believe strongly in hanging in there, suffering and enduring everything, no matter what.

Some people believe strongly that God uses the marriage as a thorn in the flesh to humble them, so, even though they may suffer, they believe staying in it is part of their ministry.

Some people believe in staying in the marriage just to protect the children from the trauma of a divorce.

Some people believe that you should remain unmarried even if your wife is dead.

Some people believe that if your wife is dead, you should not marry for at least five years, to honour her and to show that she is difficult to replace.

Indeed, it takes a strong mind of someone who is sure of himself to take such a decision to move into unchartered waters that require even more faith and attract more criticism.

5. **Some pastors are divorced because** *they believe it is the better of two options.*

What do I mean by the better of two options? Jesus taught us about choosing the better of two options.

Wherefore if thy hand or thy foot offend thee, cut them off, and cast them from thee: IT IS BETTER FOR THEE to enter into life halt or maimed, rather than having two hands or two feet to be cast into everlasting fire. And if thine eye offend thee, pluck it out, and cast it from thee: IT IS BETTER FOR THEE to enter into life with one eye, rather than having two eyes to be cast into hell fire.

Matthew 18:8-9

Jesus gave a great word of wisdom when He said, "It is better to cut off your arm and enter into heaven." It is a bad thing to go to heaven without one of your arms. But it is worse to go to hell with two arms. Jesus Christ was teaching us about how to take decisions when you are faced with two bad options.

Hard Decisions to Take: Choosing Between Two Bad Options

Divorce is always a bad option. A divorce will break your heart and break down your life. Living in a difficult marriage is also a bad experience and a bad option.

You must always take the better of the two bad options. Many ministers are often faced with two bad options. The word of God is always right. Sometimes the word of God supports both options. Sometimes both options you are faced with are biblically sound. A child of God must always follow the word of God. What about if both options are in line with the word of God? That is when Jesus' wisdom comes in. Choose the better of the two options!

Let us look at a few examples of hard decisions that Christian marriages are often faced with.

- Divorce is a bad option. It is also a bad option to live in confusion and unable to bear fruit. It is not God's will that you live in strife and confusion. God also hates divorce. So what are we going to do? It is God's will that you live in peace. It is also God's will that you bear fruit.

- Divorce is a bad option. It is also a bad option to be fighting each other, abusing each other and living in a constant state of quarrelling, strife, unhappiness, tension and stress.

- Divorce is a bad option. It is also a bad option to fight physically as a couple and embarrass yourselves in public.

- Divorce is a bad option. It is also a bad option to die prematurely because of marital quarrels.

- Divorce and remarriage is a bad option. It is also a bad option to be provoked into becoming a murderer.

• Divorce and remarriage is a bad option. It is also a bad option to be married and live as an adulterer on the side.

In your life and in your marriage, you may have to choose one of these bad options I have described above. No one can take that decision for you! No one can decide certain things for you! You have to decide which bad option you are going to take and trust that you are taking the right decision. Just expect your judgment from God at the end of the day.

When it is time for exams, no one can do them for you. You have to work out the equation yourself based on what you know. Your wisdom will be seen by the results you get in the examination. This life is an examination! Your wisdom will be seen by the decisions you take based on the options you have. Remember that God will judge you for everything you decide!

You can never say that I told you to divorce. You can only say that I told you to choose between two hard options for which you will receive your own judgment. Jesus our Saviour, decided never to get married or to have a wedding! Wisdom is justified of her children. We will find out everything we do not know when we get to heaven.

6. Some people are divorced because *they are married to a "devil"* and not a wife.

Some people simply decide that they can no longer stay with a devil. They think to themselves, "I am not in hell. Why should I live with a devil?

Even so must their wives be grave, not slanderers (diabolos) (DEVILS) sober, faithful in all things.

1 Timothy 3:11

The scripture above is very clear that wives can be literal devils. The word "slanderer" is translated from the word *"diabolos"* which means "devil". Some pastors divorce their wives because they consider their wives as literal devils and want to cast out the devil from their lives.

269

If you behave like a wife, you will be a blessing to your husband. If you behave like a devil, you greatly increase the risk of being cast away. Jesus taught us to cast out devils. When a person behaves like a literal devil it is not surprising that they are treated like a literal devil and cast out.

There are many questions a wife should ask herself. Let us go through some of them.

- Am I a wife? Am I a good wife? Am I a wife in the real sense of the word "wife"?

- Am I a help to someone's life?

- Am I complementary to my husband?

- Do I help my husband with food, clothing, finances and life in general?

- Do I satisfy my husband sexually?

- Do I live with my husband?

- Do I live apart from my husband in another house, region or country?

- Do I hinder my husband?

- Am I the one who does not show love and tenderness to my husband?

- Am I the greatest challenge to my husband's ministry?

- Am I the greatest opposition to my husband and his ministry?

- Am I the only one who argues with my husband?

- Am I the only one who does not see my husband as a great person?

- Am I the greatest accuser of my husband and his ministry?

- Am I the greatest hindrance to my husband and his ministry?

- Am I the greatest contender with my husband and his ministry?

- Am I the only one who shouts at my husband?

Depending on your answers to any of these questions, you may not be a helper to your husband at all. Indeed, you may be a devil because a devil is an opposer, a tempter, a challenger and an accuser! Remember that a wife is supposed to be a helper and not a devil. Indeed, you may only be a wife technically or even legally, but in reality you are neither a wife nor a helper to your husband.

Even so must their wives be grave, not SLANDERERS (*DIABOLOS*), sober, faithful in all things.

1 Timothy 3:11

The risk of divorce is greatly increased when you are transformed from a helper into a devil. Do not increase this risk in your life. Not all men will accept never-ending provocation! Not all men will take endless nonsense! Some men may continually accept whatever you do to them. But there are some men who will just walk away and say, "I can't take that any more."

A pastor's wife may end up being transformed from a beauty into a "devil".

What do you do with a "devil"? Cast it out!

Should you divorce from your wife? Jesus' answer is "No"! Do not separate except for adultery!

However, do remember that people will naturally tend to separate themselves from devils: (opposers, challengers, shouters, accusers, destroyers, murderers, wicked persons and adversaries). Most people would rather escape from a wicked devil than remain trapped in a room with one.

Do not become a devil: an opposer, a tempter, an accuser, a destroyer, a murderer, a wicked creature or an adversary! If you are any of these things, you put your husband in great difficulty because he is living with a devil instead of with a wife.

He can see from the Word of God that he should not separate from his wife. But his common sense tells him to separate himself from the devil that destroys him.

Do not confuse your husband nor weaken his resolve to stay with you! Do not turn into a devil or you may be cast out as an enemy!

The Lord hath taken away thy judgments, HE HATH CAST OUT THINE ENEMY: the king of Israel, even the Lord, is in the midst of thee: thou shalt not see evil any more.

Zephaniah 3:15

Do not become an accuser or you may be cast down as the accuser of the brethren was cast down.

And I heard a loud voice saying in heaven, Now is come salvation, and strength, and the kingdom of our God, and the power of his Christ: for THE ACCUSER OF OUR BRETHREN IS CAST DOWN, which accused them before our God day and night.

Revelation 12:10

Do not become an opposer! Do not contend with your husband! You will have no rest in this life if you do so.

If a wise man contendeth with a foolish man, whether he rage or laugh, there is no rest.

Proverbs 29:9

Do not make yourself into an enemy! You may be "tread upon" in your marriage.

Behold, I give unto you power to tread on serpents and scorpions, and over all the power of the enemy: and nothing shall by any means hurt you.

Luke 10:19

May God give you wisdom! May God establish you!

May God deliver you from temptation in marriage!

May your ministry never be hindered by your marriage!

May God bless you in this life! May God bless you in your adventure of marriage!